Finer

Femininity

Advent/Christmas

2014

Edited and Compiled by

Mrs. Leane G. VanderPutten

DEDICATION

This little periodical is dedicated to all the women in this
world who are devoted to making their families,
their homes, and therefore society,
a beautiful Catholic Masterpiece
in this fallen world.

CONTENTS

ACKNOWLEDGMENTS

Thank you to my husband, Vincent, for being so supportive and encouraging in this endeavor and all through our married life. ☺

1. ADVENT IS COMING!

by Leane VanderPutten

The richness of our Faith offers us so many neat traditions at this time of year!
The following quote is from Mary Reed Newland:

"Christmas is coming – for the children, the most wonderful time of the year. And for the children of Light, it should be the most wonderful, *wonder full* time of the year, because to the Church, it is the year's beginning.

No one but God could have made such a beginning, so full of beauty and glory and sheer magic as this.

But you cannot just walk into such a blaze of glory without preparation, to be ready for that sharp sweet moment when an Infant's cry cut the night "a moment's fall, the last we should know of loneliness."

You must creep up to it, think about it, count the days, watch the signs, and prepare. And folly though it seems in a world where all value is counted in material things, a child can never know the whole ecstasy of Christmas unless he knows its meaning; unless he takes its meaning into his own two hands and examines it closely and finds its mystery for himself. It must be made of his own experience and delight and love."

Do you have many Advent Traditions in your own home?

We have had many through the years. Some have dropped off, some changed, others started up. It's so fun to involve the kids in these things! We supply the magic of Christmas without having to bring in the folly of the world!

One thing we do is make a big deal about the stable. As close to the beginning of Advent that we can, we take our four wheeler out into the woods and pick up neat looking rocks, tree mushrooms, moss (depending on if there is snow covering the ground), pebbles and dirt!

Some of the years my older daughter took over the tradition of taking the younger ones out to gather stable "rubble". I was somewhat dubious as I saw them drag in **monstrous** branches that looked like half the tree! Some way, somehow, they made it work! And it was a fantastic finished product that certainly made a statement!

We cover an 8 ft. table with a mud-soaked (and dried) sheet (we've used an old tablecloth, too) and then start transforming it into.....we're not sure until it's done....but it ends up being a big and wonder-filled stable, sometimes with Bethlehem peeking from behind, sometimes not. It's a surprise and the end result is something that makes the grandchildren's eyes grow big in wonderment each time they come over!!

My married children have carried this tradition over into their own homes with their individual unique style. Some live in town so they don't have access to what nature has to offer (they come and gather things if they can) so they make their stable scene in their own distinct ways.

We don't add all the figures of the nativity right away, but do it as a gradual process with Baby Jesus "miraculously" being in His manger when we get home from Midnight Mass. (Sometimes I have to make a quick beeline to the stable after mass because I forgot Baby Jesus in the hubbub of getting ready.) ...It doesn't have to be perfect, right? :) Have fun with it....Make it special! Small things mean a lot to those little minds!

"There is also the question of time. Where do we find the time to participate in the Church's *LITURGICAL YEAR* with our children?

Like these other questions, the answer is, **we can find it if we plan for it.** We can find it quite easily by looking to see where we waste it.

Not wasting it is not easy, because the habits of *time-wasting*, although they are harmless, are hard to break - as I know from experience.

Mothers have this struggle all to themselves. It involves such things as the radio (now internet) habit, coffee breaks, long telephone conversations, chatting with neighbors, a heavy involvement in outside activities.

Somewhere most American women CAN "FIND TIME" to devote to the **enriching of their families' spiritual life.**

The *joyous discovery* is that once we have struggled and found the time, tasted and seen how sweet are these pursuits together, we begin to gauge all our doings so that THERE WILL BE TIME - because we are convinced there **must be.**" -Mary Reed Newland

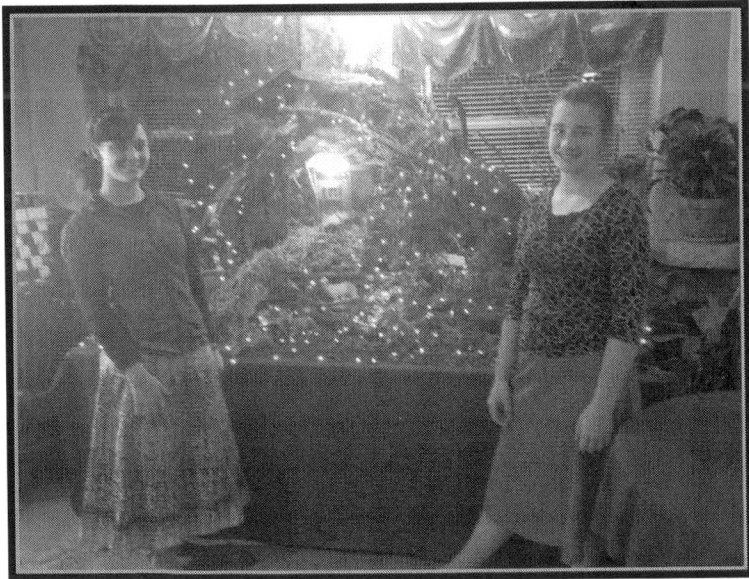

2. SOME SPECIAL FEAST DAYS IN ADVENT:

ST. BARBARA, DEC. 4TH

by Mary Reed Newland from The Year and Our Children available at Sophia Institute

The feast of St. Barbara on December 4 may seem to have no apparent connection with Advent other than the date; but it does connect, as you will see.

She is especially important to our children, and they consider it "de rigueur" to salute her on her feast day since she is the patroness of those who call for protection against lightning and electrical storms.

Frequently during the summer we have brief counsels such as, "Now stop fussing and pray to St. Barbara. She will keep us all safe and sound until the storm is over."

She was the daughter of a pagan, Dioscorus, who (according to the somewhat questionable Acts of St. Barbara) placed her in a high and beautiful tower surrounded by marvelous gardens, and sent philosophers, poets, and scholars to teach her all things.

Convinced that polytheism was nonsense, she consulted Origen, one of the most brilliant and controversial of early Christian apologists; he sent her his disciple Valentinium, who forthwith instructed and baptized her.

She thereupon threw all the statues of pagan gods and goddesses out a window of her tower, traced the Sign of the Cross everywhere on the walls, and had a third slit of a window cut in honor of the Holy Trinity.

This upset her father no end. He had her dragged out of the tower, but she somehow escaped to the mountains as he was about to slay her.

He pursued her and dragged her back by the hair of her head (which is why she is sometimes pictured being dragged about by the hair) and handed her over to Marcian, a master at the art of torturing Christians.

She was beaten with rods, torn with iron hooks, and suffered other horrible torments. To finish her off with the nicest of niceties, her father asked for the privilege of striking the final blow. He dragged her out of town and cut off her head with an axe.

The best part of the story is that, as she was being carried to Heaven by the angels, her father is supposed to have been struck dead by lightning and "hurried before the judgment seat of God." Hence her concern that we be preserved from lightning and from a sudden and unprovided death.

She is also patroness of firemen, mathematicians, firework makers, artillery men, architects, smelters, saltpeter workers, brewers, armorers, hatters, tilers, masons, miners, and carpenters, and she is invoked against final impenitence.

With this to her credit, she is precisely the saint we want supporting us in our brave resolves at the start of Advent.

So, on December 4, we sing at the dinner table, "Happy feast day, St. Barbara," and tell her story. At night prayers, we invoke her help in the words of the Collect of her Mass:

"O God, who, among the marvels of Thy power, has given the victory of martyrdom even to the weaker sex, grant in Thy mercy that we who keep the birthday of blessed Barbara, Thy virgin and martyr, may, by her example, draw nearer to Thee. Through Our Lord Jesus Christ, Thy Son, who liveth and reigneth with Thee in the unity of the Holy Spirit, God, world without end. Amen."

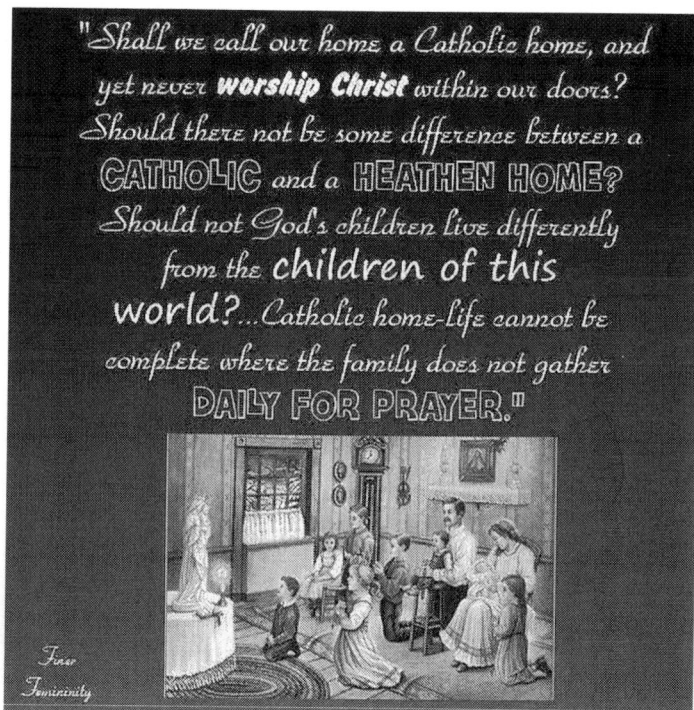

"Shall we call our home a Catholic home, and yet never *worship Christ* within our doors? Should there not be some difference between a CATHOLIC and a HEATHEN HOME? Should not God's children live differently from the *children of this world?*...Catholic home-life cannot be complete where the family does not gather DAILY FOR PRAYER."

3. ST. NICHOLAS DEC. 6TH

When my older children were young we had a lot of fun putting on a puppet show for the Feast of St. Nicholas. This was the day we gave our children stockings. We set them out on the evening of the 5th after the children were in bed. St. Nicholas Day was greeted with yelps of joy when they saw their goodies in the stockings. It was the one day they were allowed to munch throughout their lessons!

Mary Reed Newland's book gives instructions on making simple sock puppets for both St. Nicholas and Black Pete.

The following is her suggestion for a play. We used hers and added to it our own touches.

One year we did it all in poem form and another year the puppet, St. Nicholas, threw the stockings out to each child, surprising one of them with a stocking full of straw! It was my brother (he was older) and he got a big kick out of it, but it made the other kid's eyes open wide in shocked bewilderment! They were all relieved when they found out it was a joke and the recipient received his stocking after all. :)

This kind of participation will certainly make the Feast Days come alive for the children!

The following is by Mary Reed Newland, The Year and Our Children purchased at Sophia Institute Press:

Everyone assembles after dinner on December 5, the vigil of the feast, and the puppet show begins.

First, St. Nicholas appears, bowing with dignity and murmuring, "Thank you, thank you," to the shouts and clapping. He has a Dutch accent (just for merriment), and if your accent isn't all it might be, frequent interpolations of "Ja, ja" convince all present that it is superb.

"Good evening, little children," he says. "I am St. Nicholas. Ja – ja real saint I am, in Heaven now, and my feast is celebrated tomorrow. You are going to celebrate my feast? Ja? Good!

"I am not, you know, the reason for Christmas. Although I am sometimes called Santa Claus, I am not the reason for Christmas. Oh, no. Baby Jesus is the reason for Christmas. It is His birthday, Christmas, the day His Father in Heaven gave Him to all of us.

"I am waiting in Heaven, now, like you on earth, for His birthday on Christmas Day. And do you want to know something? That is why I gave gifts to little children when I was on earth! Because I was so grateful to God the Father for giving Jesus to me.

That is why we give each other presents on Christmas Day, because we are full of joy and gladness that Jesus came down to be one of us and to die to pay for our sins.

"Now, here is something you may do for my feast, and it pleases me very much. You hang your stockings tonight, and if you are very good children, you will get cookies in them!

"But if you are bad…. Ahhh, if you are bad, you will get – not cookies – but straw! Black Peter will put straw in your stockings."

Up pops Black Peter, giggling and snickering and wagging his hands at the audience, which promptly rolls on the floor and shrieks.

The bishop is grave. "Peter! Peter! Behave yourself, or I will have to use a switch on you! Peter, you are going to put straw in some stockings? Jah?"

Peter looks coy, cocks his head, and makes odd noises that say neither aye nor nay.

"Ah, he will not tell. Peter, be fair now. No straw for the good children, you know. But be honest as well – straw for the naughty ones!"

Peter snickers again, wags at the children, then turns and throws himself on the bishop, arms around his neck, mewing noisily.

As the bishop nods his head paternally, Peter slyly turns to the children, waves a free arm and giggles. Then he quickly buries his head in the bishop's shoulder again.

After this you can have Peter sing a song or two, and the bishop can end the play with a hymn and lead the children in a little prayer or two, asking for the grace to be good and to love little Jesus with all their hearts. Then it is all over.

All go rushing about looking for stockings, full of high hopes for cookies – which, of course, they have spent the afternoon helping to make (or seen Mother buy).

13

The following morning tells the tale, and it is sometimes a mixture of fun and bittersweet. We have a little friend named Teddy who was unable to bear the suspense; so he bade his sister look in his stocking for him.

When she reported, "Cookies!" he was so amazed (what with the weight of his past sins pressing so hard upon him) that he gasped, "Are you sure?"

Advent is the beginning of the **NEW LITURGICAL YEAR.** *It is a season of spiritual preparation, marked by eager longing for the coming of the* **Savior through grace at Christmas,** *and for His second and final coming. It is also an ideal time to establish in our homes* **liturgical customs** *which will* ***restore our children to Christ.***

-Helen McLoughlin

4. THE REASON FOR CHRISTMAS PRESENTS AND THE IMMACULATE CONCEPTION, DEC.8

by Mary Reed Newland

Why are we making gifts for each other two, three, four weeks ahead of time? Working as hard as we can to make something beautiful? To wrap it beautifully? To tie it beautifully? To think of something full of love to write on the card that goes with it? Because we know that Christmas is coming.

That Jesus should become man and save us from our sins is more than good reason to prepare, to anticipate. We want everything to be perfect for Jesus and for our beloveds when Christmas comes.

Just so, God the Father prepared for the coming of Jesus. He prepared for His divine Son a perfect Mother through whom He could come into the world. This is how He prepared: God the Father knew that when the time came, from our Lord's death on the Cross would flow graces that would never end, that would make it possible for Godlike powers to be given to men.

For example, He knew that our Lord would institute a sacrament through which grace would come to wash away the Original Sin inherited from Adam and Eve, and to fill the soul with marvelous beauty where God Himself could dwell.

In creating a Mother for His Son, God used this grace ahead of time – not to wash away Original Sin but to make a Mother whose soul was untouched by Original Sin. This is what we mean when we speak of Mary's Immaculate Conception, the name she used for herself when at last she told St. Bernadette who she was.

God does not live in time. He invented time for us so that we could keep track of ourselves, but He has no need of it, and in the foreverness of Heaven, He used all the magnificent graces His divine Son poured forth from His death on the Cross in time to merit for our Lady a perfect soul from the instant He breathed it into being.

That is why, when Gabriel came to her in Nazareth, he could say, "Hail, full of grace…." That is why, when Mary went to visit Elizabeth, Elizabeth could cry out, "Blessed art thou among women…."

This does not mean that our Lady was conceived in a miraculous manner, as her divine Son was conceived. She was born of the lawful union of Joachim and Anne, loving husband and wife. It does mean that at the moment the seed of life that was to become our Lady was united to her immortal soul, it was to a soul God had created perfect.

Our Lady was made immaculate so that when the time came for the plan of the Redemption to unfold, her pure and holy body would be a perfect resting place wherein the love of God – His Holy Spirit – would breathe and His divine Son would begin to live. This beautiful doctrine explained to the children on the vigil of her feast will help form the spirit in which the entire family will assist at the Mass in her honor and receive Holy Communion.

The great Advent mysteries in the life of our Lady relate in many ways to the knowledge we must give our children about their bodies. Now we see again why we must have reverence and awe for our bodies. They are made for great and holy things.

All the little girls in the world who will grow up to discover that God's will for them is to be wives and mothers will, as mothers, carry their babies the way our Lady carried her baby. Every mother we see who is expecting a baby can remind us of our Lady. It is so good of God to have His Son come to us this way, and so sanctify the bearing of babies. He could have come in thunder and lightning. He could have come like a wild storm riding the sun, driving the moon and the stars before Him.

But, loving us in our littleness and our struggles and our pains and worries, He chose to be like us in all things save sin, so that we would always know that God knows what it is like to be a man.

If we have children for whom it is time to learn something of the way babies are born, Advent is an especially appropriate time to continue with that part of sex instruction.

This carrying of babies within the mother's body, is it not beautiful? This is how our Lady carried her Baby, close to her heart, protected and sheltered there by her own pure body. This delivering of babies, as we call it – the emergence of the baby from his mother's body – is it not wonderful? It is God's way.
He decided it was to be like this. If there was a finer way for it to be, He would have it be that way.

"Let us pray tonight and ask our Lady to help us have reverence for our bodies, and for the bodies of others, and never to do anything with them God does not want us to do." These things and a host of others relating to the meaning and spirit of Advent make beautiful, rich, prayerful conversations that go with the making of gifts.

Some are for parent and child alone, some for the group; both ways, the treasury to explore is inexhaustible.

FAITH ★ FAMILY ★ FRIENDS

Working on Christmas gifts:

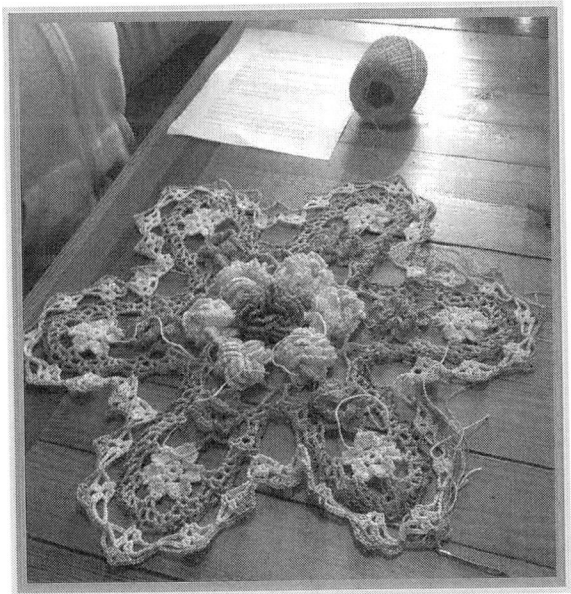

5. THAT FAVORITE CHRISTMAS NOVENA, THE ST. ANDREW NOVENA, NOV. 31ST

The Christmas Novena, also called The St. Andrew Novena is one of the most popular Catholic Advent prayers.

Our family loves to say this novena each year in preparation for Advent. We offer it up for intentions that we have discussed beforehand….family intentions….and then each one may privately add their own intentions.

Because the prayer is longer than 9 days, and not quite 27, it's technically not a novena or a set of novenas, but, because it is prayed 'novena style', that is, repeatedly for a set amount of days, it is referred to as a novena.

In our family, we have found that we remember to say the novena best when we attach it to our daily Rosary. It takes a bit of extra time, probably the length of a decade of the rosary, so therefore adds a little extra sacrifice on top of it....always a good thing, right?

The prayer can be said at any time during the day but it would be best to make it a regular time so as not to forget it. If you happen to forget a day (which we have) we do two sets of the prayer the next day. It would be better not to forget at all but sometimes life isn't that way. So do the best you can.

Imagine a child who loves you...he is willing to do just about anything in his power to please you. The Christ Child is ready to answer our prayers. He has the power to do and to give us anything, and He will, as long as the petitioned favor isn't contrary to what Our Lord deems necessary for your eternal salvation.

In this Advent season of preparing for Christ's coming, the St. Andrew Christmas Novena is a loving way to prepare ourselves and our families.

St. Andrew holds the honor of being the first apostle to be called by Christ to follow Him.

This novena is a bit different in that it does not invoke the intervention or aid of the saint himself, but is adoring, glorifying the hour of Christ's birth and seeking aid from God Himself!

The novena is begun on the Feast of Saint Andrew, November 30th, and is said through Christmas Eve, December 24th.

St. Andrew Christmas Novena

Hail and Blessed be the hour and the moment in which the Son of God was born of the most pure Virgin Mary, at midnight, in Bethlehem, in piercing cold.

In that hour, vouchsafe, O my God, to hear my prayer and grant my desires through the merits of Our Savior Jesus Christ and of His Blessed Mother. Amen.

Recite 15 times per day.

6. THINGS I WISH I'D KNOWN
CHARLOTTE SIEMS

www.charlottesiems.com

Charlotte Siems is a devoted wife and mother of 12. She has some sound advice here:

Woulda, coulda, shoulda. Regrets about what we should have done can overwhelm us. Life is an education, and all of us can look back and see things we wish we'd done differently.

Moms especially can have a hard time with regrets. There is a time for asking forgiveness and a time for doing the best you can moving forward. A productive use of regrets is to pass on the lessons we've learned to other mothers, in the hopes that it will help them avoid some future heartache.

Hence, this short, incomplete list of some things I wish I'd known as a young mother.

Things I Wish I'd Known

- **Little ones sleepily crawling into my lap during my so-called private devotional time was a short season.** My frustration at not getting me-time was short-sighted. Welcoming them with open arms and gratefulness would have served us better.

- **Children are definitely potty-trained** by the time they leave for college.

- **My kids would learn to read**, even if it wasn't on the timetable of other people and institutions.

- **I didn't have to go with every thought that popped into my head.** I didn't have to be ruled by the emotions created by random thoughts, and I didn't have to keep thinking them.

- **What was going on inside my head was reflected on my face.** Too often I greeted my husband with a frown or met my children's eyes with a harsh look.

- **People remember how you made them feel.**

- **Most, if not all of the time, my husband meant well.** He didn't have a hidden agenda, he didn't mean to hurt my feelings or neglect me. He loved me beyond what I could accept at the time.

- **I could have made my needs known** rather than stuffing them and nursing wounds and getting resentful.

- **I should have taken better care of myself physically.** Sometimes I wish I would have had tools like the "T-Tapp" exercise program back when I was a young mom, rather than gaining 100 pounds and feeling beyond exhausted most of the time. But then I wouldn't have had a story to encourage others.

- **I could choose what kind of day I would have.** I didn't have to let events and other people rule my mood.

7. FORMING GOOD HABITS/THE ART OF SELF-DENIAL – REV. GEORGE KELLY

Advent is a great time to talk about self-denial!

Forming good habits.

Your need to direct your child's actions should diminish in proportion to his age. It will do so if you establish good habits of living which enable him to fulfill his obligations as a matter of course. By instilling good habits, you can impress upon your child that he has obligations to God and family; that authority demands his respect; that he must be reverent at his religious duties, cooperate in the home, and sacrifice his own interests where necessary for the welfare of others.

By developing good habits in many different areas of life, your child will strengthen his character. He will get many of these habits simply by watching you. From you he should learn to accept his responsibility toward Church, country and family.

He should begin the habit of contributing to the support of your pastor at an early age, and be responsible for putting a small sum in the collection plate each Sunday. He should be taught to tip his hat in reverence when he meets a priest or sister. He should also bow his head when he hears the name of Jesus. Many similar habits can be developed.

In the home, he also can learn habits of responsibility at an early age. As soon as he is able, he should do some work around the house as his contribution toward family living. The boy or girl of seven may set the table for dinner or remove the dishes after it. A youngster of nine or ten can help vacuum the floors and keep his own room in order. The older girl can wash dishes and prepare meals occasionally. The older boy can maintain the lawn and wash the car. By performing all these tasks in a regular fashion and without being bribed to do so, your children learn the habit of contributing to the common welfare.

Habits can be inculcated so that they become part of the daily pattern of living. The youngster who is taught to say his morning and night prayers will soon say them automatically, his parents will not have to remind him every day. Similarly, the youngster who is required to do his homework every evening after dinner develops a regular pattern of performance. It will become an automatic process. When he arrives at high school, he will be able to take responsibility for his studies entirely.

The art of self-denial.

One of the most important things you can do for your child's development is to teach him to practice self-denial willingly. If he is to become successful as a human being, he must learn to deny himself immediate pleasures to achieve a future good. We must all deny ourselves to achieve eternal happiness in heaven. So too on a worldly level. The husband and wife who fail to deny themselves at least some material pleasures during their early years of marriage will reach old age penniless and dependent upon others.

The student who cannot deny his impulse for pleasure when homework assignments must be done, pays the price ultimately by failing in his studies and finding that he cannot achieve a suitable station in life.

Learning to say no is therefore the most important single lesson that your child must learn. During his lifetime, he must say no to temptations that besiege him on all sides; he must say no to discouragements, defeatism and despair; if he is to reach any stature in the spiritual or even worldly order, he must say no to urges to take things easy, relax, or give up the fight. For this reason, parents who try to do everything for their child ultimately do nothing for him; by preventing him from developing self-discipline and the ability to say no, they prevent him from acquiring the most important attribute of a complete person.

How can you teach your child to practice self-denial? Mainly by setting up rules for his conduct and behavior and adhering to them firmly. When you do this, you make him aware of penalties that he must pay unless he controls impulses of one kind or another. Must he be home for dinner every night at 6 P.M. or lose desserts for a week? He must then say no to playmates who urge him to play another game of ball that will last beyond the designated time. Must he maintain a certain scholastic average or spend extra hours at his books each day until the next marking period? He will then learn that it is easier to deny himself to achieve passing grades now than to make greater sacrifices later.

The concept of self-denial appeals to youngsters. It represents a challenge--an opportunity to prove their mettle as strong-willed boys and girls. When they learn how to win over their lower instincts, they prepare themselves in the best possible way for the greater challenges and battles they will face as adults.

JOY ★ PEACE ★ LOVE

*When a child is given to his parents, a crown is made for that child **in Heaven**, and woe to the parents who raise a child without consciousness of that **eternal crown!***
-Archbishop Fulton J. Sheen

8. ST. NICHOLAS VS SANTA CLAUS

By Mary Reed Newland

On December 6 comes the feast of the Christmas saint, St. Nicholas, although most of our celebration of this feast comes on his vigil, December 5.

We find a puppet show a delightful way to tell his story, explain his relation to the Christ Child, and introduce the hanging of stockings for his feast day.

St. Nicholas was really a Turk born in Asia Minor. For a long time he was Bishop of Myra (near the southern coast of Turkey to the right of the Island of Rhodes – in case you look for it on a map).

An orphan, he grew in love of God, became a priest, and made a pilgrimage to the Holy Land to venerate the places of our Lord's life.

On the voyage, a terrible storm threatened to sink the ship, but by his prayers all were saved. For this reason he is venerated as patron of boatmen, fishermen, dock workmen, and sailors.

Returning to his native land, he was made a bishop; his generosity and love for the poor and for children, as well as his many miracles, endeared him to Christian people all over the world.

He is also venerated as the patron of scholars, coopers and brewers, travelers and pilgrims, those who have unjustly lost a lawsuit, and as patron and annual benefactor of schoolchildren (especially boys), and is invoked against robbers and (in Holland) for protection of seafaring men.

Many legends surround St. Nicholas, among them the one saint story I personally cannot abide: the tale of the three little boys murdered and salted down in a tub is too much. We never tell it.

The story we like best is the well-known tale of the three marriageable daughters who were nevertheless unmarriageable for want of dowries. Hearing of their plight, the saint went silently by their house one night and tossed a bag of gold through the window for the oldest, who not long after found a husband for herself with no trouble at all.

Then he crept by a second time and tossed a bag of gold through the window for the second daughter, who likewise was suddenly at no loss for suitors. As he was about to toss the gold through the window for the third daughter, the father of the girls caught sight of him.

Throwing himself at his feet, he thanked him, confessed his sins, begged his blessing. Plainly it is from this story that the tradition has grown wherein St. Nicholas is said to leave gifts, candies, and sweets on windowsills, in shoes, and even in the stockings of good little children.

It is the Dutch diminutive Sinter Klaas ("Sant Nikolaas") that became, by way of the New Amsterdam Dutch, the familiar American Santa Claus.

It is among the Dutch also that we find the appearance of Black Peter, his page, who follows him, distributing switches, coal, straw – whatever – to the naughty children as St. Nicholas gives treats to the good. Black Peter appeared in the Dutch festival after the invasion of Holland by the Spaniards, who brought black servants with them.

"Telling the truth about Santa Claus" need not rob children of their Christmas magic. It adds to it with another feast to celebrate, another saint to know and love, another emphasis gently persuading them to meditate on the coming of the divine Child.

And if we really fear to take away that part of it which is surprise, that marvelous moment Christmas morning when the presents are at last mysteriously there, be assured the little ones continue to pretend.

Our littlest ones, knowing the truth, continue to pretend that it is all assembled in the most mysterious and magical fashion.

"But – then – who gives us the presents?" children will ask.

"Who loves you most in all the world gives you the presents."

"Who is that?"

"You guess."

They screw up their faces, think hard. Then suddenly all brighten: "You – and Daddy, and Grandma and Granny!"

It is like the circle that never ends. God loves mothers and fathers and gives them children they will love, and they teach the children about God, and the children love God, and since God wants them all with Him in Heaven, He sends His Son who loves them so much that He gives up His life for them, and that is so much love that it pays for their sins and buys back Heaven for them....

At Christmas everyone is so happy about all this that we all give each other presents. Shouldn't that be the reason we give and receive presents?

It would be a little embarrassing to be asked, "Don't you think the Christ Child is an adequate substitute for Santa Claus?" and feel you must answer no.

He really is and He must become the all of Christmas for families who are going to try to live lives of deep faith. It is not really worth it to toss in this "little white lie" when we are trying so hard to teach children impeccable truthfulness.

Probably not all children who discover there is no Santa, when they have been told by their parents that there is, will consider their parents dyed-in-the-wool liars, but there is the danger that they will discount some of every other truth they are taught. This is an age when accuracy and unadorned truthfulness are not particularly in vogue.

Yet a concern to speak the utter truth in everything will teach a child better than anything else how to be utterly truthful himself, how to be honest with his own conscience – which is the same thing as being honest with God.

Santa Claus is not a serious lie, but St. Nicholas in his rightful place, gazing with us at the Christ Child, is a much lovelier truth.

One thing, however, it is not cricket to do: go about the neighborhood telling all the children who do believe in Santa Claus that "there is none."

This kind of revelation is guaranteed to leave nothing but heartache behind. Without proper explanation or background, it is really cheating a child of something he dearly loves.

Most children can learn to keep their own counsel about this; where there is disparity on the subject in the neighborhood, with love and tact the mothers can explain and help prevent unpleasant exchanges.

One of the traps into which most parents of goodwill eventually fall before Christmas has arrived is to shout in the heat of some shortness of tempers: "How do you expect to get presents on Christmas if you aren't good now?"

No sooner are the words out of your mouth than you could bite off your tongue. But it has been said. The ugly implication is there: you might not get presents for Christmas.

St. Nicholas's feast is an ideal time for straightening out this problem of being good and not being good before Christmas. It is true that the issue should have something to do with the end result, but when we threaten this way, we forget that the reason God the Father sent the Christ Child wasn't because everyone had been good, but because they hadn't been good. To transfer the burden of the "be good or else" problem to St. Nicholas is infinitely more comfortable.

Here the threat involves no more than a stockingful of cookies, but it is a prospect sufficiently dreadful to give them pause. It also involves a happy solution to the naughtiness. No good behavior – no cookies. It usually works (I speak from experience).

The shock of seeing that you meant what you said, of hearing St. Nicholas warn you the night before and discovering he meant what he said, is most salutary.

Most *enfants terribles* will stand dolefully watching the more virtuous munching their cookies and make a superb effort to mend their ways, and yet the event is not of such magnitude that it leaves any permanent scars.

People always ask how we handle the delicate business of sharing should this occasion produce one or two malcontents without cookies. We are all, of course, very sad to see they have no cookies, but if it is a warning and a punishment, then it is a warning and a punishment.

Character training is involved, and also your own authority. No cookies – shared or otherwise.

9. WHERE ARE YOU GOD AND HOW COME YOU'RE NOT HELPING OUT?
by Leane VanderPutten

I love Christmas time. I love all the rich traditions, the beauty surrounding it, the music, the love and camaraderie of good friends.

But I also know it can be a very hard time for some. They can be extra lonely at Christmas, they are sick, they are missing someone close to them who may have recently died.

Christmas has a way of increasing that suffering, because the hardship is such a contrast to the beauty and joy of the season.

We may find ourselves saying, "Where are You, God, and how come You're not helping out?"
How many times in *my life* have I use these words...or at least words of this sort?

We have black times when we pray and pray and pray and our petitions seem to be falling on Deaf Ears. Sometimes we might even find ourselves getting angry at God.

Every time I reacted this way, I regretted it. The dust would settle and I would see most clearly how God was working in that situation or how incredible blessings had followed a very painful situation.

My mom always told me to thank God even in adversity, *while going through it*.....thank Him when things look so murky and it looks like you or your loved ones had been abandoned.

That's not an easy thing to do!! It's definitely an act of the will. But I remember the saying that goes something like this, "The devil trembles most when a person gets on their knees *in spite of the fact* that everything within him rebels ."

So I have learned through the years that, first of all, there *will* be dark times. That is the way life is. It has its sufferings. Period. We truly wouldn't want it any other way. It is the Royal Road of the Cross.

I have learned also that these times are special because this is when I am sharing in His sufferings in just a little way…. a way that I know is pleasing to Him.

I also try to think about the many great sufferings of others, the sufferings of the persecuted in the Middle East (which is something we can't even imagine in our day and age) and those who are suffering big things closer to home.

My own sufferings, though *real and hurtful*, (and God understands that) are nothing compared to these other sufferings. What a great reason to thank God!

And then the thing I have learned, finally, is to be grateful to God *for the difficulties themselves*. Days of darkness will go by and I will forget.. I will writhe in pain and look for ways to get out of it. I will pray, do extra holy hours or whatever I think I need to be doing. I know these are all good.

But then the light bulb goes off and I remember to THANK HIM for exactly what it is I am going through! I believe this is very pleasing to Our Lord.

I know that in hindsight I will be looking back and saying, "I thank You God for that situation and all the good that You have brought from it for me and for others."

So whatever you're going through today, whatever hardships you have during this Christmas season especially, take a moment to thank God for them. Give them as a gift to the Baby Jesus.

The light is always at the end of the tunnel and you don't want to be guilty for shaking your fist at God. This is one time you DO want to "jump the gun" and "count your chickens before they are hatched." You want to believe and KNOW that God is the Author of all and will turn this into good for you and for your family. You want to take a moment to thank Him who is a most loving Father. He sees everything that we are going through. He WILL come. He's shown us that many times in our lives, hasn't He? Remember, He has the hairs on our heads counted.

That's not just a cute cliché, that has a world of meditation in it. Meditate on it, believe it and live it this Christmas season!

From Father Jacques Philippe:

Finally, we shouldn't forget the sort of obedience that may be the most important and the most overlooked: what might be called "obedience to events." This notion obviously poses a difficult theological and existential problem.

"Obedience to events" does not mean falling into fatalism or passivity, nor does it mean saying that everything that happens is God's will: God does not will evil or sin. Many things happen that God does not will. But he still permits them, in His wisdom, and they remain a stumbling block or scandal to our minds.

God asks us to do all we can to eliminate evil. But despite our efforts, there is always a whole set of circumstances which we can do nothing about, which are not necessarily willed by God but nevertheless are permitted by him, and which God invites us to consent to trustingly and peacefully, even if they make us suffer and cause us problems.

We are not being asked to consent to evil, but to consent to the mysterious wisdom of God who permits evil. Our consent is not a compromise with evil but the expression of our trust that God is stronger than evil.

This is a form of obedience that is painful but very fruitful. It means that after we have done everything in our power, we are invited, faced with what is still imposed on our will by events, to practice an attitude of abandonment and filial trust toward our heavenly Father, in the faith that "for those who love God, everything works together for good."

To give an example, God did not want the treachery of Judas or Pilate's cowardice (God cannot want sin); but he permitted them, and he wanted Jesus to give filial consent to these events. And that is what he did—"Father, not what I will, but what thou wilt."

The events of life are, after all, the surest expression of God's will, because there is no danger of our interpreting them subjectively. If God sees that we are docile to events, able to consent peacefully and lovingly to what life's happenings "impose" on us, in a spirit of filial trust and abandonment to his will, there can be no doubt that he will multiply personal expressions of his will for us through the action of his Spirit who speaks to our hearts.

If, however, we always rebel and tense ourselves against difficulties, that kind of defiance of God will make it difficult for the Holy Spirit to guide our lives. What most prevents us from becoming saints is undoubtedly the difficulty we have in consenting fully to everything that happens to us, not, as we have seen, in the sense of a fatalistic passivity, but in the sense of a trusting total abandonment into the hands of our Father God. What often happens is that, when we are confronted with painful occurrences, we either rebel, or endure them unwillingly, or resign ourselves to them passively.

But God invites us to a much more positive and fruitful attitude: that of St. Thérèse of Lisieux, who, as a child, said: "I choose it all!" We can give this the meaning: I choose everything that God wants for me. I won't content myself with merely enduring, but by a free act of my will; I decide to choose what I have not chosen.

St. Thérèse used the expression: "I want everything that causes me difficulties." Externally it doesn't change anything about the situation, but interiorly it changes everything. This consent, inspired by love and trust, makes us free and active instead of passive, and enables God to draw good out of everything that happens to us whether good or bad.

Do not anticipate the unpleasant events of this life with apprehension, rather anticipate them with the perfect hope that, as they happen, God, to whom you belong, WILL PROTECT YOU.

Fr. Jacques Phillippe

QUIPS 'N' QUOTES

My God, the **birth of the Lord** *gives rise to a thousand* THOUGHTS AND AFFECTIONS *in our hearts! Never could there have been a* POORER OR A HAPPIER BIRTH, *nor at the same time a more* **radiant and happy mother!**

Saint Paula preferred to live as a **pilgrim in Bethlehem** *than as a* **society lady in Rome,** *being convinced that day and night in this hospice where she was staying she could hear the cries of the little* SAVIOR IN THE CRIB.

As Saint Francis of Assisi used to say of the little **Infant of Bethlehem,** *He inspired him to* **despise greatness and earthly ambitions,** *summoning him back to the sublime* **love of abjection.**

-St. Francis de Sales

10. GIVING OF YOURSELF THIS ADVENT

Mary Reed Newland reminds us of the richness of the season of Advent and how we can make it come alive for us and for our children!

Here's a great story reminding us that God wants US this Advent, with all our personalities and our talents, with all our foibles and quirks. He loves us for who we are!

From The Year and Our Children:

"Next, there is the all-important matter of a birthday gift for the Light of the World. If there are to be gifts for others, there must first be a gift for Him. It is His birthday, not ours; and what kind of birthday is it when all the gifts go to the wrong people? What kind of gift would He like?

There is a story to tell at the beginning of Advent, about someone who had nothing to give. It illustrates best of all for children how the intangible is to God the most tangible, and makes entirely reasonable to them a scale of values one would suppose far over their heads.

The story is "The Juggler of our Lady." It is as old as old, but each time it is told, it seems more beautiful.

It is about a monk who had no great talents, who could not illuminate manuscripts or write music or sing songs or paint pictures or compose prayers or do any of the dozens of things the other monks were preparing to do in honor of the Mother of God and her newborn Son.

So he made his way to the crypt below the main altar of his abbey church, and there before her statue, he humbly confessed that he had nothing to give. Unless ... but of course. He had been a tumbler and a juggler in the world. Long ago. He had been a rather brilliant tumbler and juggler, if the truth were known. Might she like to see him juggle and tumble?

She was young and happy. She had laughed and clapped her hands. Surely her Child had. Perhaps he could tumble for them, all alone in secret? That is what he would do: give her the only thing he had to give. He would display his talent for the honor and glory of God and the entertainment of the Queen of Heaven.

So he removed his habit down to his tunic, and then he danced. And he leaped and he tumbled and he juggled in the most inspired fashion until finally he fell in a swoon at the feet of his Lady. And while he lay there limp and wet from his efforts, senseless as though he were dead, she stepped down from her pedestal and tenderly wiped the sweat from his brow and sweetly considered the love he had put into this performance for her and her dear Son's sake.

And this happened every day.

Now, there was another monk there who began to notice that the tumbler came not to Matins and kept watch on him because "he blamed him greatly."

So he followed closely the movements of the tumbler. One day he followed behind him and carefully hid himself in the recesses of the crypt and witnessed the whole performance. So profoundly was he impressed and inspired that he hied himself straight to the abbot, who prayed God would let him, too, witness this wonder of dancing and juggling for the Mother of God.

And he did see not only the dancing and the juggling and the leaping and the capers but also the Queen of Heaven, in the company of angels and archangels, come down and with her own white mantle fan her minstrel and minister to him with much sweetness.

When it came to pass that the abbot made it known to the minstrel that he had been seen – poor minstrel! He fell to his knees to beg forgiveness and plead with them not to send him out from the monastery.

Which, of course, they did not do but held him in high esteem until the day he died, and there about his bedside they saw the Mother of God and the angels of Heaven receive his soul and carry it to everlasting glory.

"Think you now that God would have prized his service if that he had not loved Him? By no means, however much he tumbled…. God asks not for gold or for silver but only for true love in the hearts of men, and this one loved God truly. And because of this, God prized his services."

This, then, is the pattern for the gift: it must be a giving of self.

Our children usually give Him their desserts and treats during Advent except on Sundays, the two feasts, and the two birthdays that we celebrate with special festivities.

These days they give Him something else instead. They try to give more willingly than before their bumps and hurts, and (this really hurts) their will in such matters as being first, sitting by the window in the car, licking the bowl, doing the dishes without being asked, or doing homework first instead of last.

No funnies (especially no Sunday funnies) makes a beautiful gift for the funnies and comic-book addicts, and no radio for the radio fans. No TV is an excruciatingly difficult gift to make but more beautiful for its being difficult; and the Christ Child has a way of giving back more than you have given Him.

Ultimately we must insist on times of quiet, away from the manufactured entertainments of this world, in order to form the habit of recollection.

We are supposed to be contemplatives according to the capacity God has given us – which means that we see the world, ourselves, and all that is created in the right relation to God and that we think on these things often with love.

Whether we will end up "contemplatives" in cloisters or as contemplatives who are farmers, writers, bus drivers, policemen, dancers, whatever – in order to grow, we must be reaching constantly to God with our minds.

We need quiet for the very least of this, for the beginning of meditation. Parents can begin the process for their children, especially in this wonderful season of Advent!"

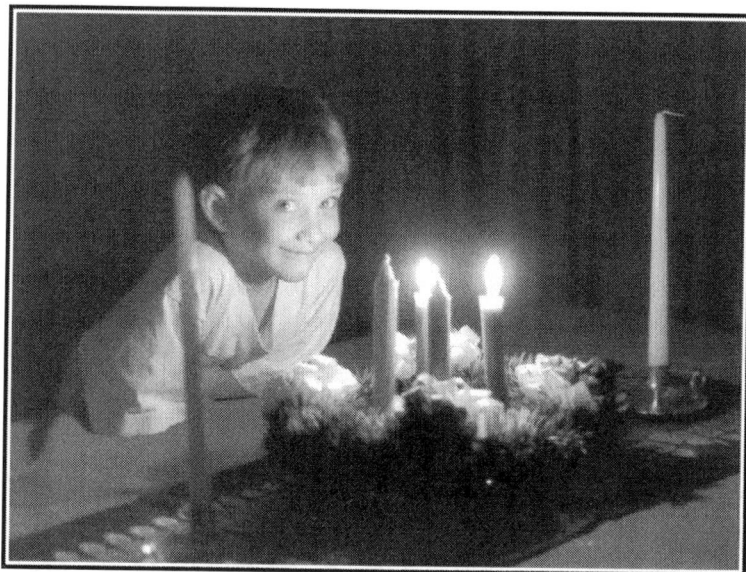

QUIPS 'N' QUOTES

MAINTAINING PEACE IS LINKED TO THE PRACTICE OF SILENCE. THIS SILENCE IS NOT AN EMPTY SILENCE: IT IS *peace*, ATTENTIVENESS TO GOD'S PRESENCE AND *attentiveness to others*, WAITING IN TRUST AND HOPE IN GOD.

WE SOMETIMES LET OURSELVES BE OVERTAKEN BY EXCESSIVE NOISE—NOT SO MUCH PHYSICAL NOISE AS THE *ceaseless whirlwind of thoughts, imaginations, and words* THAT WE'VE HEARD OR SAID—AND ALL THIS MERELY FEEDS OUR WORRIES, FEARS, AND FRUSTRATIONS, AND OBVIOUSLY LEAVES THE *HOLY GHOST* LITTLE CHANCE OF MAKING HIMSELF HEARD.

SILENCE IS NOT EMPTINESS BUT THAT GENERAL ATTITUDE OF INWARDNESS THAT ENABLES US TO HAVE AN "INNER CELL" IN OUR HEART, TO USE AN EXPRESSION OF ST. CATHERINE OF SIENA'S, WHERE WE ARE IN GOD'S PRESENCE AND *converse with him.*

SILENCE IS THE OPPOSITE OF THE DISSIPATION OF THE SOUL IN CURIOSITY, GOSSIP, AND SO FORTH. IT IS A CAPACITY FOR *returning almost spontaneously within ourselves*, DRAWN BY THE PRESENCE OF GOD WITHIN US.

-Fr. Jacques Philippe

11. A MERRY CHRISTMAS TEA

I think it would be a great idea to have a Tea Party for one of the Twelve Days of Christmas! Girls and Boys alike enjoy tea parties...and older folks, too! And it would be a great opportunity to pull out the nice china (mine is sparse but that's ok) and set a real spread! We love tea and tea parties over here! We don't take time to have them too often but it is always a good time!

You can plan a tea party of your own.....simple or a little more extravagant, with a little help from Emilie Barnes.

-Emilie Barnes, Christmas is Coming; Our Holiday Family Organizer

Christmas is a special time for friends and family to gather together, and a Christmas tea offers a wonderful chance to celebrate your relationships and the season itself. Let your Christmas tea be your special gift to friends, family, and yourself.

Tea parties are more personal than a general party. There is something about a tea party that brings out the best in people – the best behavior, the best intentions, the best attitudes. We expect a little more of each other when we come to tea, and we tend to live up to those expectations. We give a little more. That in itself is cause to celebrate!

I begin planning my holiday tea party in October, because it takes time to get the details just right. Keep your eyes out for pretty Christmas-themed notecards with no message inside to use for invitation. Send them out by the end of November.

There are no limits on the decor for a tea party. Take advantage of the wonderful decorating materials that are available – sparkling red and green fabrics, lush and fragrant greens, and all kinds of candles. Fragrant pine garlands, red berries, shiny red apples, pretty ornaments, poinsettias and anything Christmassy are great for an arrangement or special centerpiece.

The table can be as decorative as you like. I usually pull out all the stops and use my best china and fancy white linens for this celebration. I love to decorate each guest's plate with a little candle held in a special clip – the same kind used many years ago in Europe to secure little candles on the Christmas tree. There are no rules to decorating. It's whatever sets a tone and mood for your party. Play Christmas music to add to the merriment!

And load the table with a variety of sweet and savory foods. I usually have a special tea, some tea sandwiches, a fancy cake, fruits and a special cheese like mascarpone, and decorated Christmas cookies. Everything is presented on doily-lined trays…it's almost too pretty to eat!

The most special part of this holiday tea is when we share our favorite memories and Christmas blessings together. I light the candle of the person nearest to me and ask her to share a Christmas thought or Christmas blessing. After she speaks. she lights the candle of the person next to her, who then shares her Christmas thoughts. Around the room we go with each person sharing a bit of her heart.

Spiced Christmas Tea

Ingredients

- 2 medium oranges
- 1 medium lemon
- 4 cardamom pods
- 4 whole cloves
- 4 teaspoons English breakfast tea leaves *or* other black tea leaves
- 4 cups boiling water

Directions

- Using a citrus zester, remove peel from oranges and lemon in long
- narrow strips. (Save fruit for another use.) Place the peel strips,
- cardamom and cloves in a large bowl. With the end of a wooden spoon
- handle, crush mixture until aromas are released.
- Add tea leaves and boiling water. Cover and steep for 6 minutes.
- Strain tea, discarding peel mixture. Serve immediately. Yield: 4 servings.

Almond Chicken Tea Sandwiches

3 boneless, skinless chicken breasts, cooked and chopped coarsely

1/2 cup slivered, blanched almonds

1/2 cup mayonaise

White or wheat bread

Butter each slice of bread well. On half the slices, spoon about 3 tablespoons of almond chicken mixture. Top with remaining slices.Wrap in wax paper and again in a slightly dampened kitchen towel. Let filling set for at least an hour before serving. Cut off crusts and trim into pretty shapes.

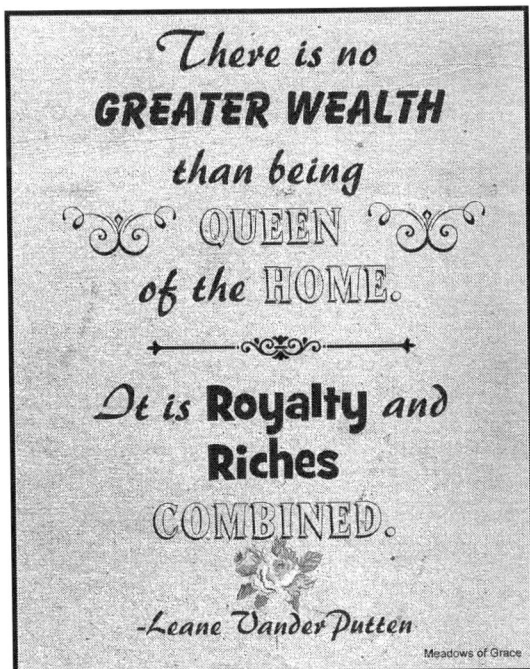

There is no **GREATER WEALTH** than being *QUEEN of the* HOME.

It is **Royalty** *and* **Riches** COMBINED.

-Leane VanderPutten

Meadows of Grace

12. A SPIRITUAL CHRISTMAS CRIB

This activity/devotion is something we have done throughout the years. It is a beautiful little observance preparing our hearts for the coming of Our Lord at Christmas.

You can do the special activity indicated each day in this devotion in your own manger scene, using your imagination.

Or you can do what we did. We put up 4 big white poster board papers on an empty wall to make a *big* blank paper just waiting for the crayons and sharpies to make their mark! (You can make it as big or small as you like, using just one or two poster boards.) Each day we draw the part of the manger scene that is applicable to that day.

I usually do the drawing in pencil then the child chosen for the day traces it with colored markers and colors it in.

We also print out all of the special prayers individually and put each one up for the day so we can say the prayer throughout the day.

We sometimes forget a couple days and have to back track. It doesn't have to be perfect. It is a wonderful family devotion that helps to make Advent and Christmas meaningful!

Here's the Directions for the Devotion, starting on Dec. 1st:

Read the thought indicated
about Christ's first crib.
Practice it during the day. Do this daily during
December and make your heart a worthy crib for
Christ on Christmas Day.

DEC.1 – THE STABLE
Frequently during the day offer your heart to the little Infant Jesus. Ask Him to make it His home. *-Sweet Jesus, take my heart and make it meek and pure.*

DEC.2 – THE ROOF
See that the roof of the stable is in good condition, so that the Infant Jesus is protected from rain and snow. This you will do by carefully avoiding every uncharitable remark. *–Jesus, teach me to love my neighbor as myself.*

DEC.3 – CREVICES
Carefully stop every crevice in the walls of the stable, so that the wind and cold may not enter there. Guard your senses against temptations. Guard especially your ears against sinful conversations.*–Jesus, help me to keep temptations out of my heart.*

DEC.4 – COBWEBS
Clean the cobwebs from your spiritual crib. Diligently remove from your heart every inordinate desire of being praised. Renew this intention at least three times today. *–My Jesus, I want to please You in all I do today.*

DEC.5 – FENCE
Build a fence about the crib of your heart by keeping a strict watch over your eyes, especially at prayer. *–Sweet Jesus, I long to see You.*

DEC.6 – MANGER
Fix the best and warmest corner of your heart for the manger of Jesus. You will do so by abstaining from what you like most in the line of comfort and amusement. *–Mary, use these sacrifices to prepare my heart for Jesus in Holy Communion.*

DEC.7 – HAY
Supply the manger of your heart with hay, by overcoming all feelings of pride, anger or envy. *Jesus, teach me to know and correct my greatest sins.*

DEC.8 – SOFT STRAW
Provide your manger with soft straw by performing little acts of mortification; for instance, bear the cold without complaints; or sit and stand erect. *–Dear Jesus, Who suffered so much for me, let me suffer for love of You.*

DEC.9 – SWADDLING CLOTHES
Prepare these for the Divine Infant by folding your hands when you pray, and praying slowly and thoughtfully. *–Jesus let me love you more and more.*

DEC.10 – BLANKETS
Provide the manger with soft warm blankets. Avoid harsh and angry words; be kind and gentle to all. *–Jesus, help me to be meek and humble like You.*

DEC.11 – FUEL

Bring fuel to the crib of Jesus. Give up your own will; obey your superiors cheerfully and promptly. *–Jesus, let me do Your will in all things*

DEC.12-WATER

Bring fresh clean water to the crib. Avoid every untruthful word and every deceitful act. *–Dearest Mary, obtain for me true contrition for my sins.*

DEC.13 – PROVISIONS

Bring a supply of food to the crib. Deprive yourself of some food at mealtime or candy as a treat. *–Jesus, be my strength and nourishment.*

DEC.14 – LIGHT

See that the crib has sufficient light. Be neat and orderly about your person; keep everything in its place in your room. *–Jesus, be the life and light of my soul.*

DEC.15 – FIRE

Take care to have the crib of your heart warmed by a cozy fire. Be grateful to God for the love He has shown us in becoming man; behave with grateful respect towards your parents and relatives. *– Jesus, how can I return Your love; how can I show my gratitude to You?*

DEC.16 – THE OX

Lead the ox to the crib. Obey cheerfully without making excuses and without asking "why." *–I will obey for love of You, Jesus.*

DEC.17 – THE DONKEY

Bring the donkey to the crib. Offer to the Divine

Infant your bodily strength; use it in the service
of others. *–Jesus, accept my service of love;
I offer it for those who do not love You.*

DEC.18 – GIFTS
Gather some presents for the Divine Infant and
His Blessed Mother. Give alms for the poor and say
an extra decade of the rosary. *–Come, Jesus, to
accept my gifts and to take possession of my heart.*

DEC.19 – LAMBS
Strive to bring some little lambs, meek and
and patient. Do not murmur or complain.*–Jesus, meek and
humble of heart, make my heart like Yours.*

DEC.20 – SHEPHERDS
Invite the shepherds to pay homage to our newborn
King. Imitate their watchfulness; stress in your
speech and thoughts the idea that Christmas is
important because Jesus will be born again in
you. *-Jesus, teach me to love You above all things.*

DEC.21 – THE KEY
Provide the stable with a key to keep out
thieves. Exclude from your heart every sinful
thought, every rash judgment *–Dear Jesus, close
my heart to all that hurts you.*

DEC.22 – ANGELS
Invite the angels to adore God with you.
Cheerfully obey the inspirations of
your guardian angel and of your conscience. –
*Holy Guardian Angel, never let me forget that You
are with me always.*

DEC.23 – ST. JOSEPH
Accompany Saint Joseph from door to door. Learn
from him silently and patiently to bear refusals

and disappointments. Open wide your heart and beg
Him to enter with the Blessed Virgin Mary.
–Saint Joseph, help me to prepare for a worthy
Christmas Communion.

DEC.24 – THE BLESSED VIRGIN
Go meet your Blessed Mother. Lead her to the
manger of your heart and beg her to lay the
Divine Infant in it. Shorten your chats and
telephone conversations and spend more time today
thinking of Jesus and Mary and Joseph.
–Come, dear Jesus, Come; my heart belongs to You.

The beginning of our Christmas stable to the finished product:

13. CHRISTMAS TRADITIONS – OLD AND NEW

Traditions become so much a part of what our children will remember as "home". They will carry these customs with them as they strike out on their own. It will fill their own lives with a depth and richness that only family, faith, home and traditions can bring.

That is what I love about our wonderful Faith – filled with beauty and traditions.

Christmas time can be such a time of lovely customs, also. Maybe Emilie Barnes will spark a new one today.

Christmas Is Coming: Our Family Holiday Organizer

A rich heritage can be passed on from generation to generation with the special traditions that are part of your Christmas celebration, and it's not too late to start now. It makes no difference whether you're a family or an individual – you can still create wonderful memories and establish special traditions. "Let this Christmas be one of happiness, and the New Year be radiant with hope and filled with the impulse of doing something for somebody every day. "

Cookie Exchange – This is a great idea! Who invented it? We're not really sure, but it was truly a stroke of genius! Instead of making a variety of cookies for the holiday, you can make a large batch of your favorites and swap them for many different kinds.

I received an invitation that instructed me to bring seven dozen cookies plus my recipe written on a recipe card that would be displayed by my cookie plate.

We drank hot Christmas tea and wrote down other recipes on pretty cards from our hostess. Each guest received a paper tote bag (a box or tray could also be used) to take our wonderful collection of goodies home.

Christmas Memory Book – An album dedicated to remembering Christmases is a great idea. All this tradition requires is a photo album. With each year a photo could be added, with the Christmas card sent for the year, and a journal detailing Christmas festivities and traditions. Children may add little mementos if they wish as well.

Family Movies, Video, Slides – It's so much fun to see those old family movies, slides, photos or videos. Set aside an evening to do just that. It's interesting to see how everyone has changed.

Take a family Christmas photo every year too. We take ours at Thanksgiving. It's the one time we all seem to be together. Coordinating your clothing is also fun. Be creative and do your own thing. Include the pets, teddy bears, and favorite dolls or toys as well. Some of the photos we have of past Christmases delight our grandchildren because their parents are hugging dolls and teddy bears!.

Enjoy Christmas Cards – Ours begin to arrive early in December. We store them in a basket as the days draw closer to Christmas. Then, beginning January 1, we take our card-filled basket to our meal table, and before or after our meal, each member of the family draws out a card. We read the card and who it is from and then offer a prayer for that person or family. This tradition can last well into the new year.

Give Toys – Many local and civic organizations provide an opportunity for individuals and families to donate toys for distribution to needy families on Christmas Eve. What a great way to teach your children the Joy of Giving.

Adopt a Family – There are many opportunities where your family can adopt a family in need. Help them with holiday food and gifts – it's a great bridge-builder. This can be done anonymously if it would be easier.

Put up a "JOY" Stocking – During the month of December, each family member puts thoughts, love notes and prayers in the "joy" stocking. Then on Christmas Eve or Christmas Day, the notes are pulled out and read.

Some of my own thoughts on Traditions:

The Spiritual Christmas Crib – This is a wonderful devotion and fun activity for the whole family starting at the beginning of Advent. (see page 50).

The Twelve Days of Christmas - Lovely practice that keeps the Spirit of Christmas alive following Our Lord's Birthday on Christmas.

The Manger – Besides our Nativity Scene, we make a rather large manger out of twigs or Popsicle sticks and a glue gun. We then cut up pieces of yellow construction paper into small strips for straw. Each time one of the children make a sacrifice they put their name on one of the pieces of straw and put it in the manger. On Christmas morning Jesus will have a soft bed to lay on….we hope!

Christmas Traditions Don't Have to Be Expensive -Emilie Barnes

1. Go caroling around the neighborhood or at a convalescent home to spread cheer. Bring a thermos of hot cocoa to keep everyone warm.

2. Attend a Christmas pageant and take lots of pictures.

3. Enjoy the holiday lights in your hometown on a nighttime walk. It's fun to see your neighbor's decorations.

4. Go to a recital at a local church. Many choirs sing The Messiah and other seasonal music.

5. Have a special hot chocolate time, use Christmas mugs. Sprinkle the tops with little marshmallows, whipped cream, and colored sprinkles. Use a candy cane to stir. Yum!

6. Throughout the year, save the remnants of candles from special occasion (birthday, anniversaries, special dinners, etc.). Melt the remnants for one large Christmas candle.

7. Look at garage sales, flea markets and antique spots for pretty inexpensive teacups to place homemade tea cookies, candies or tea bags in. Give them with gifts along with a message:

"When this cup is empty and the goodies are all gone,

Fill it again for another friend, so you can pass it on."

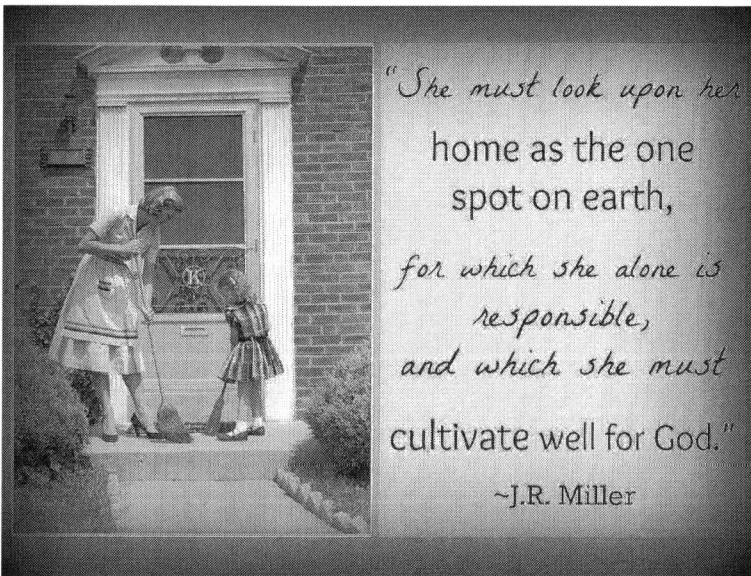

"She must look upon her home as the one spot on earth, for which she alone is responsible, and which she must cultivate well for God."

~J.R. Miller

14. CHILDREN AND CHRISTMAS – CHRIST IN THE HOME, FR. RAOUL PLUS, S.J.

IT IS easy to understand how enraptured children can become at the contemplation of a tiny Babe in a manger. To have God reduce Himself to their own status, to become a child like them, to need a mother, what more could they desire! They feel on a footing with Him. The Almighty is of their stature!

We are told that on Christmas Eve, Saint John of the Cross used to carry a statue of the Infant Jesus in procession about the monastery. The procession would stop before each monk's cell asking hospitality for the Divine Babe. The cells, like the hearts of the monks, would open to faith and to love. Only then would the statue be carried to the Crib and the Divine Office begin.

Children share the simplicity of these holy monks. Nothing attracts them more than the Crib. This very attraction makes it imperative that they learn about it correctly.

Care must be taken not to mix in with the gospel mystery any details which the child will later come to recognize as false.

What good can come of representing Santa Claus almost as God the Father who has given us His Son? Why let children believe that it is the Infant Jesus Himself who comes down the chimney to bring them presents . . . only to hear some day, "You know, mamma, this is the last time I'm going to believe in Little Jesus who comes down the chimney with presents."

If we mix the false with the true, it is no wonder the child will not be able to separate legend from doctrine later on. The Gospel is sufficiently extraordinary in itself without our adding any of our own creations to it. If we do, we may well fear the child will become disgusted later at being deceived and reject everything.

Any charming legend or pious little story we may want to tell them when they are very little should be kept quite distinct and handled very differently from the dogmatic truths and authentic historical facts we teach them.

Let us not introduce fairies into the story of Joan of Arc's childhood, nor put the legend of Saint Nicholas rescuing little children on a level with the realities of the Redemption, with the facts of Our Lord's saving us from hell.

If, therefore, we are to capitalize on the child's attraction for the marvelous, let us avoid abusing his credulity; above all when dealing with the lives of the saints, with the Blessed Virgin and with Christ, let us not mix the false with the true.

Let us always keep on a plane apart those truths which are to be forever the object of ineradicable belief.

There is, however, a positive suggestion to offer: Explain to the child how Baptism has made him a living Crib; not a wooden manger padded with straw, but a living Crib; not a crib where only little Jesus lives but a Crib where the Three Persons of the Holy Trinity dwell, the Three Divine Persons.

Here, too, is splendid opportunity to show the child the difference between the two presences— the presence of God in the soul through grace and the presence of Jesus in the stable through the Incarnation.

15. CHRISTMAS TIDBITS FROM MARY REED NEWLAND

Holy Mother Church is very wise. She knows us better than we know ourselves.

For this reason, she designs her year with unerring instinct.

She begins rather than ends with Advent and Christmas, for life makes no sense except in the view of eternity — and the key to eternity for us is the Redemption.

Advent is a four-week condensation of the four thousand years mankind waited for the Redemption. It's our time to reflect on the meaning of Christ's coming, to long for it, to purify ourselves so that we'll be ready.

It's a penitential season, with penance done with joy. The lighting of the Advent wreath, the family praying together nightly in its presence, the weekly ritual of candle-lighting to remind us of His coming (He who is the Light of the World) — these rites are sermons in themselves.

Since on Christmas He will be a birthday Child, He must have birthday presents; and the family chooses mortifications to make beautiful gifts for Him.

The feast of St. Nicholas is December 6, the time for learning about Santa Claus. No rival to Christ, this saint, but one of the elect waiting in Heaven as we do on earth for the glory of His birthday to break over the world.

Fun with St. Nicholas, stockings filled with cookies for children who are good, is a reminder of the reason we give and receive gifts.

He gave out of his love for Christ and His little ones, out of gratitude to God, who gave Christ to him.

The feast of St. Lucy, on December 13, is the day for a feast of lights, for thinking of the Child who is Light, for planting the Christmas wheat. Sprouted, soft green by Christmas, it reminds us of our daily bread, the bread of life on our altars, the end of the story that has its beginning at Christmas.

All through the weeks of Advent, the harvest of mortifications increases, counted with little beans in tiny boxes, or with straws in an empty crèche. The children watch self-denial fill the gift box, make a soft bed in the crèche; every day passed means one day closer to His birthday.

Christmas Day the Beloved is here, tiny, helpless, newborn. The crèche is His throne, and we are like shepherds, invited to adore. Gifts are given and received because we are the pampered children of God to whom He gives the gift of His Infant Son.

Following Christmas come the days when we greet and honor witnesses to His glory: St. Stephen, St. John the Evangelist, and the Holy Innocents. Then comes New Year's.

Now the Church reminds us to look back at the sins of the past, and forward with holy hope to the opportunities of the future, and calls us to the altar to pledge our good intentions at the Mass that celebrates His Circumcision, the day He received His beautiful name.

Help your child to grow holier through liturgical celebration. The liturgical year is a cycle unfolding from life to death to glory.

Observing it year after year, joining Christ with our love, our wills, and our understanding, we live the union of member to Body, no longer branches of the vine that are dead. We are living, bearing fruit — or at least aspiring to.

How can one be any closer to Christ? Perhaps it sounds easy, this living the liturgical year. Or perhaps it sounds impossible. It's neither. But it's slow. It will come to us, and we will grow in it only as fast as the Spirit allows.

It's not just a matter of pasting over our lives with liturgical stickers. Its outward forms — its Advent wreaths and crèches and Christmas bread, its candles and blessings, its penitential purple and ashes and palms, its stories and customs and celebrations — are nothing if interiorly we're not on fire with its spirit.

It's the reality of Christ's life, and it cannot be separated from the struggle to grow Christ-like. It's the same old struggle to love, be kind, grow in patience, work well and play well, to please God in everything we do.

But it's supported now by the graces loosed every day by the prayer of the Church. That's the big difference. Living liturgically, we're really united to Him, praying the prayer of His Church.

Raising children liturgically, we're using all the treasure at our command. We asked the children, "How do you feel about being Catholics?"

They answered, "Oh, being Catholics is fun! You have feasts, and saints, and stories, and things to do — and when you go to Mass and Father holds up our Lord, you say, 'I love You!' "

16. GIVE YOUR LOVED ONES THE GIFT OF COURTESY THIS CHRISTMAS

-by J.R. Miller

A secret of happiness in married life is courtesy. By what law of nature or of life is it, that after the peals of the wedding bells have died away, and they have established themselves in their own home, so many husbands and wives drop the charming little amenities and refinements of manner toward each other, that so invariably and delightfully characterized their interaction before marriage?

Is there no necessity for these civilities any longer ? Are they so sure now of each other's love, that they do not need to give expression to it, either in affectionate word or act? Is wedded love such a strong, vigorous and self-sufficing plant that it never needs sunshine, rain or dew?

Is politeness merely a manner that is necessary in interaction with the outside world, and not required when we are alone with those we love the best? Are home hearts so peculiarly constituted, that they are not pained or offended by things that would never be pardoned in us, if done in ordinary society?

Are we under no obligations to be respectful and to pay homage to our dearest friends— while even to the rudest clown, or the greatest stranger, which we meet outside our own doors— we feel ourselves bound to show the most perfect civility?

On the contrary, there is no place in the world where the amenities of courtesy should be so carefully maintained, as in the home. There are no hearts which hunger so, for expressions of affection, as the hearts of which we are most sure. There is no love which so needs its daily bread—as the love that is strongest and holiest.

There is no place where rudeness or incivility is so unpardonable, as inside our own doors and toward our best beloved! The tenderer the love and the truer— the more it craves the thousand little attentions and kindnesses which so satisfy the heart!

It is not costly presents at Christmas and on birthdays and anniversaries, that are needed; these are only mockeries— if the days between are empty of affectionate expressions.

Jewelry and silks will never atone for the lack of warmth and tenderness. Between husband and wife there should be maintained, without break or pause— the most perfect courtesy, the gentlest attention, the most unselfish amiability, the utmost affectionateness!

Coleridge says, "The happiness of life is made up of minute fractions, the little soon-forgotten charities of a kiss or a smile, a kind look, a heartfelt compliment, and the countless infinitesimals of pleasurable thought and genial feeling ."

These may seem trifles, and the omission of them may be deemed unworthy of thought; but they are the daily bread of love, and hearts go hungry when they are omitted.

It may be only carelessness at first in a busy husband or a weary wife— which fails in these small, sweet courtesies, and it may seem a little matter— but in the end the result may be a growing far apart of two lives which might have been forever very happy in each other— had their early love but been cherished and nourished.

"We are not drawn to God by iron chains, but by sweet attractions and holy inspirations."

-St. Francis de Sales

17. CATHOLIC TRADITIONS FOR ADVENT AND CHRISTMAS – MICHAELANN MARTIN

Michaelann Martin has 9 kids, the youngest , almost 7 months, has down Syndrome. She can be contacted to speak through "focus" www.focus.org

Issue: How can families better live the spirit of Advent and Christmas in their homes?

Response:

The Catholic Church has designated the four weeks preceding Christmas as Advent, a time to "prepare the way of the Lord" for His coming as our King and Savior. In addition, the Church teaches that:

When the Church celebrates *the liturgy of Advent* each year, she makes present this ancient expectancy of the Messiah, for by sharing in the long preparation for the Savior's first coming, the faithful renew their ardent desire for his second coming. By celebrating [John the Baptist's] birth and martyrdom, the Church unites herself to his desire: "He must increase, but I must decrease" (Catechism, no. 524; original emphasis).

By participating in various time-honored traditions, such as making Jesse trees or putting on a Christmas play at home, Catholic families can engage more fruitfully in the seasons of Advent and Christmas.

Discussion:

"Either we live the liturgical year with its varying seasons of joy and sorrow, work and rest, or we follow the pattern of the world," writes Helen McLoughlin in *Advent and Christmas in a Catholic Home,* commenting on the challenge Catholics have of being "in the world but not of the world" throughout the year. She wrote these profound words in the 1950s, but they are even more important today because of the general decline in Catholic family life during the last 40 years. With two parents working in many households, there is less time to devote to the spiritual life of the family. As Catholic parents, we must readjust our priorities and teach our children by living our faith, both inside and outside the home.

It seems fitting that Advent is the beginning of the liturgical calendar, for it is a season of spiritual preparation marked by an eager longing for the birth of Our Savior Jesus Christ. There are age-old Advent practices which will help our children and families live closer to Christ. The practices are time-tested and proven. They teach the doctrine of redemption and develop a sense of generosity toward God (cf. Catechism, nos. 2222-26). A family's strong and living faith will become their heritage and a mode to reinforce the religious practices centered in the liturgy.

"Children love to anticipate," writes McLoughlin. "When there are empty mangers to fill with straw for small sacrifices, when the Mary candle is a daily reminder on the dinner table, when Advent hymns are sung in the candlelight of a graceful Advent wreath, children are not anxious to celebrate Christmas before time. That would offend their sense of honor. Older children who make Nativity sets, cut Old Testament symbols to decorate a Jesse tree, or prepare costumes for a Christmas play will find Advent all too short a time to prepare for the coming of Christ the King."

These are hopeful thoughts as we prepare to incorporate some of these liturgical activities into our home life during Advent to enable us to truly celebrate Christmas. It is a shame that many do not fast during Advent, because without a fast there can really be no feast at Christmas. Fasting and other forms of penance, such as prayer and almsgiving, help to purify our hearts and prepare us for the celebration of Christmas (cf. Catechism, no. 1434).

The Church especially encourages participation at weekday Masses during Advent, because in the Eucharist we find the source and goal of our Advent preparation: Christ Himself, whose sacrifice reconciles us with God (cf. Catechism, no. 1436; Sacred Congregation of Rites, *Eucharisticum Mysterium*, no. 29).

The Church primarily celebrates Christmas from Christmas Day until the Solemnity of the Epiphany, which commemorates the manifestation of Christ as the Savior of the whole world (cf. Mt. 2:1-12). The Church has also traditionally celebrated Christmas for 40 days, culminating on the Feast of the Presentation (Feb. 2). During this time, the birth of Christ is celebrated as one continuous festival. It is just as important to celebrate during the Christmas season as it is to prepare for Christ during Advent.

The following activities are provided so that you and your family can live Advent and Christmas to the fullest.

Advent wreath: The Advent wreath, which has German origins, is probably the most recognized Advent custom. It is a wreath made of evergreens that is bound to a circle of wire. It symbolizes the many years from Adam to Christ in which the world awaited its

Redeemer; it also represents the years that we have awaited His second and final coming. The wreath holds four equally spaced candles, the three purple ones lit on the "penitential" Sundays and a pink one for Gaudete, the joyful third Sunday in Advent. There are many available prayers and hymns found in the reading list that can accompany your personal Advent wreath ceremony.

The Empty Manger: Each child may have his own individual manger, or there may be one manger for the whole family. The idea is that when acts of service, sacrifice, or kindness are done in honor of Baby Jesus as a birthday present, the child receives a piece of straw to put into the manger. Then, on Christmas morning, "Baby Jesus" is placed in the manger. Encourage your children to make Jesus' bed as "comfortable" as possible through their good deeds. In the process, explain Christ's incomparable self-gift at Christmas and Easter that enables us to be part of God's family.

The Jesse tree: The Jesse tree tells about Christ's ancestry through symbols and relates Scripture to salvation history, progressing from creation to the birth of Christ. The tree can be made on a poster board with the symbols glued on, or on an actual tree. For further information read, *Advent and Christmas in a Catholic Home.*

St. Nicholas Day: The feast of St. Nicholas is on Dec. 6th. It is a highlight of the Advent season. Each child puts out a shoe the night before St. Nicholas Day in the hope that the kind bishop — with his miter, staff, and bag of gifts — will pay a visit. The current "Santa Claus" is modeled after St. Nicholas, but commercialism has tarnished the true story. Many families give gifts on both Dec. 6 and Christmas. Read about St. Nicholas in your favorite saints book.

The Christ candle: Any large white candle can be used for the Christ candle. The idea is to decorate it with symbols for Christ. Use old Christmas cards, sequins, holly, etc. The candle can be lit on Christmas Eve to show that the Light of the World has arrived. Then continue to light the Christ candle throughout the year at

Sunday dinner to remind your family of our waiting for Christ, as well as celebrating His birth and Resurrection.

The Mary candle: Some families have the custom of decorating the Christ candle with a blue veil on December 8th, the Solemnity of the Immaculate Conception. On this great feast, others place a candle with a blue ribbon before a statue or picture of the Blessed Virgin, whose "yes" to God enabled our Lord's coming at Christmas. The candle is lit during meal times to serve as a delightful reminder of Mary's eager expectation of the "Light of the World." It can also serve as a reminder to each family member to keep their own light of grace burning as a preparation for Christ's coming.

St. Lucy Cakes: The feast of St. Lucy, virgin and martyr, is on December 13th. This marks the opening of the Christmas season in Sweden. Her life story can be found in most saints books, as can the recipe for the traditional cakes. The symbolism is rich and her life story worthwhile reading.

The Nativity scene: This is the event in which the entire family shares — setting up the Christmas manger. Mary and Joseph should be far off traveling and their approach to Bethlehem can be adjusted daily. Older children can make life-size Nativity models, carve them, cut them out from cardboard, or set up pre-made figurines. The creative ideas are without limit. Make sure to place the Nativity scene where many can admire the children's efforts to give God glory.

Christmas Baking: There are many recipe books available to find great traditional Christmas baking ideas. The baking usually starts around December 20th. As Christmas approaches, the house will smell of baking and fresh wreaths. The glory of Christmas is at hand! Move the manger to a focal point, add lights to the Nativity to be lighted on Christmas Eve, and anticipate together.

Blessing of the tree: More and more frequently families are blessing their Christmas trees. It is good to remind children that "the tree" relates to many aspects of our faith. For example, we are reminded that our first parents were not allowed to eat from one tree, and that Christ paid the great price for our redemption by hanging on a tree (cf. Acts 5:29-32).

There are many different stories which attempt to explain why we use a tree at Christmas. For instance, St. Boniface in the eighth century gave the balsam fir tree to the Druids in place of the oak tree, the symbol of their idol. He said, "The fir tree is the wood of peace, the sign of an endless life with its evergreen branches. It points to heaven. It will never shelter deeds of blood, but rather be filled with loving gifts and rites of kindness."

There are more stories and blessings included in McLoughlin's *Advent and Christmas in a Catholic Home*. A family can also participate in Advent through daily Mass, the Liturgy of the Hours, or at least by following the weekday Mass readings at home, as the Church anticipates her Savior's coming, and then His early life following Christmas. A family that participates together in Mass and other activities during the Advent and Christmas seasons will grow closer in Christ — "The Reason for the Season" — and give a great witness to friends and relatives.

"Father, all-powerful God, your eternal Word took flesh on our earth when the Virgin Mary placed her life at the service of your plan. Lift our minds in watchful hope to hear the voice which announces His glory and open our minds to receive the Spirit who prepares us for His coming. We ask this through Christ our Lord. Amen."

FAITH ★ FAMILY ★ FRIENDS

18. MY LITTLE STORY ABOUT THE ROSARY

By Leane VanderPutten

Give the gift of a resolution to say the daily rosary to the Christ Child this Christmas....and continue it throughout the year!

I'm a slow learner.

Sometimes it just takes me a long time to "get" some things.

At the "tender " age of 20, the Rosary and the Consecration to Our Lady (St. Louis de Montfort style) was what set my feet on solid ground in a world that spun around me with all sorts of "answers" to life's problems. And I wanted answers.

My friends were leaving the Catholic Church that was rocked by liberalism and they were going to greener pastures. It was all beckoning to me. The Catholic Church I attended didn't seem to hold out any answers. I had attended a Catholic School and went to Mass every Sunday all my growing up years. I was involved in youth groups and church choirs. And yet I didn't know about the

True Presence until I was almost 20 years old! There was an emptiness…. but I didn't know what the problem was.

Then something happened. I went to a few classes on St. Louis de Montfort's True Devotion to Mary. I didn't like them but I stepped out in faith and began by saying a decade of the rosary each day (while my thoughts traveled to those naysayers saying "repetition of words are useless…dumb….they also said…IDOLATRY…you can't pray to Mary) but I persevered…..And then I consecrated myself to Our Lady…(once again, the horrible doubts and misgivings…) I did it anyway. It was not very comfortable.

I met hubby. We began our courtship and our marriage with the rosary…daily. It was a commitment. It wasn't wonderful…or beautiful…. It was a **commitment**.

We had children. Many children. We said the rosary. So often, it seemed fruitless. Life was so distracted, so wrought with the everyday little crosses and duties…but it was a commitment and we stuck to it.

I knew it was a good thing. I knew Our Lady asked for the Family Rosary at Fatima: "I am the Lady of the Rosary. Continue always to pray the Rosary every day." I believed. I was committed. *Hubby was always committed.* :)

I see now the fruits. I look around at a very crazy world and thank God through tears for what He has given to us…through no merit of our own.

I know that we could have really messed up. We were two people coming from very different backgrounds….both very strong-willed. We made our mistakes…..but we had the rosary. And we stuck with it, day in and day out, year after year.

A family that prays together, stays together. I know that is not everything. If we have an open heart, the rosary gives us the graces to make the necessary changes as we need them.

The Daily Family Rosary. Steady, Constant. Amid the crosses of daily life with many children, the misunderstandings between husband and wife, the financial burdens…we had the rosary.

When the kids got hurt or sick, when I was very ill, when hubby was in the hospital and we had no money to pay, through tragedies, accidents and fires, when I didn't understand why God was letting things happen to us…. we were saying the rosary.

Steady and constant, we prayed it every day, amid slouching kids, tired husband, cranky, pregnant wife.

Thank God for that rosary. I know my life is not done yet. We still have children at home, children who can….and will….make a lot of mistakes. But for the record, they all (married ones, too) put their faith first, amid their own struggles. They say the daily rosary and it will be what holds them together through thick and thin.

If you have troubles, say the rosary. If, amid your noisy and boisterous family, you are suffering loneliness, say the rosary. Do you have fears and worries? Say the rosary. Are your rosaries dry and distracted?…Keep saying it.

Truly, who knows better than Our Lady, *Our Mother*, our humanness, our failings, how small we are, how distracted we are. She will help. Persevere. Don't give up.

It is just now that I am beginning more to understand the beauty, the mystery, the deep, interior, spiritual growth that can take place through the rosary. Like I said, I am a slow learner.

I am glad that God is very, very patient.

He has given us a very special gift. Don't take it for granted and don't go a day without saying it!

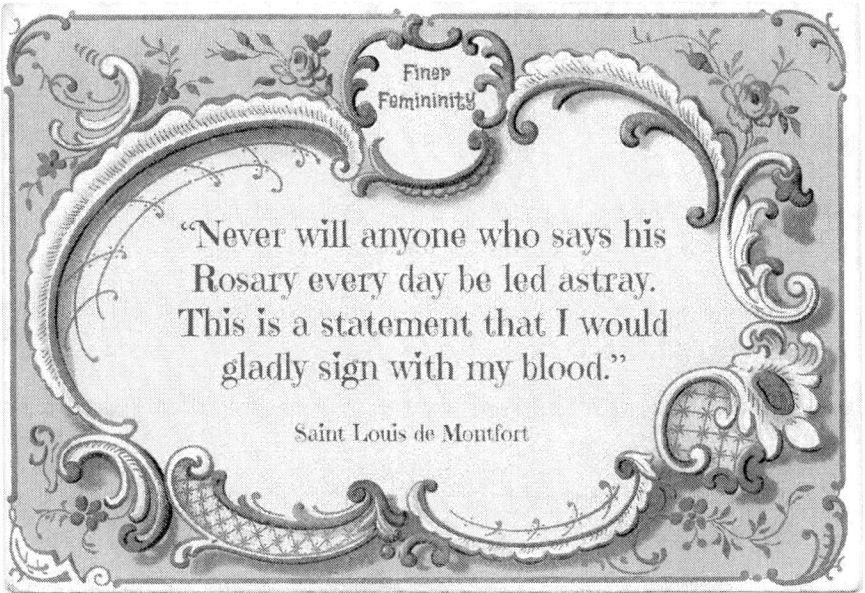

"Never will anyone who says his Rosary every day be led astray. This is a statement that I would gladly sign with my blood."

Saint Louis de Montfort

19. NATALIE'S TWELVE DAYS OF CHRISTMAS

*The thing that I especially like about this practice is that it helps to make the Christmas Season festive **after** Christmas has arrived...when all the songs have stopped on the radio, the decorations taken down, the tree thrown out and hearts begin to appear as we anxiously await Valentine's Day. (eyes rolling)*

From Natalie:

When my husband and I first started our family we had lots of gifts under our tree. As our family grew the number really grew overwhelming and really meaningless; plus we wanted to do more than just Advent calendars and wreaths and then a pile of gifts on Christmas Day.

In the midst of feeling this way I came across a Catholic blog talking about how they celebrated the 12 days of Christmas. Nothing real detailed: just how they gave out little gifts each day instead of all of them on Christmas Day; spending that time as a family and enjoying each other's company. So I started searching the internet, pulling together ideas and coming up with a new way; one focused on celebrating Christmas throughout the entire 12 days (through Epiphany) and also linking it to our deep Catholic culture and calendar.

I came up with a plan to focus more on family and our faith and less on THINGS. I would wrap one item having to do with the activity for the day, and we would do that family activity on that day of Christmas. The kids weren't sure what some of the activities were, so they would be guessing all day long based on the vague items in the box. So there was a present for each day under the tree. I tried to link the Catholic Calendar with what we were doing as well. Obviously from year to year the wrapped items change, but as an example of how last year went:

Christmas Day: The kids got to open the one individual gift we gave each of them, the few relative's gifts and their stockings (if you do St. Nicholas Day then you would not do stockings, obviously!). We always make sure that even though we now have 9 kids, they each have something special from us. It didn't need to be expensive, but one thing that they really would love.

Dec. 26th: This is St. Stephen's day. Traditionally, this was called "boxing day" because Catholics would gather together a box of items and donate them in honor of St. Stephen, who was known for his charity. So for this day I wrapped up an EMPTY box and the kids gathered together some "stuff" to give to a charitable organization. We talk about gratefulness and looking outside of ourselves to those who are in need of help.

Dec. 27th: Last year we did "Ice Cream Sundae Day". I had some neat toppings that we never have and a few types of ice cream. There was not a huge focus on the saint of the day (St. John), but more of a fun family activity. I wrapped up 4 different toppings and some cherries in the box. Their guesses of what this day was about were quite cute.

Dec. 28th: The Feast of the Holy Innocents. We said a special rosary for life this evening; but we also just spent time with our kids making Gingerbread Cookies. We made a point to give some to our mailman as well so that the kids would not only have fun, but also serve others who are not always thanked for the every-day things they do to serve others in their occupation. I wrapped up some cookie frosting for this day. This year we will be attending a semi-formal Christmas Dance, so I'll probably put the kid's dress shoes in the box instead. ☺

Dec. 29th: Feast of the Holy Family. We did a "coloring" day. I wrapped up some neat, detailed coloring books from Dover. We wanted to focus on peaceful activities and this was one. We made a point to spend much of the day coloring with them and they really enjoyed doing it with us.

Dec. 30th: One of our many December birthdays. So we kept it simple: we boxed up some wall decals as a family gift and the kids enjoyed decorating walls and sharing/trading different stickers among themselves.

Dec. 31st: Today we boxed up a movie and popcorn. The kids had never seen The Hobbit so they were super excited to see that in there. I didn't just want it to be media; so we also made popcorn balls out of the popcorn and then enjoyed them with our movie that evening.

Jan. 1st: Mary Mother of God. Since today was a Holy Day, I made a feast and labeled it "tidbit day". We made a lot of little things: olives, cheese, salami, a punch bowl, little crackers, cookies and veggies. We found some unusual items in the international aisle of the grocery store. The kids drank their punch out of fancy glasses and we had little plates. I wrapped up hand-made name tags for the kids, a Christmasy candle for the centerpiece and candy cane napkins.

Jan. 2ⁿᵈ: Feast of St. Basil and Gregory, who were good friends. In honor of that I wrote little thank-yous to all of the kids, telling them how much I appreciated different things about them. I also put notebook paper in the box so they could write to each other. Then at the dinner table we read them aloud to each other and talked about true friendship and how to choose friends wisely, how to be a good friend, etc... We also made a point to pray the 2ⁿᵈ Joyful mystery of the rosary when Mary visited Elizabeth.

Jan. 3ʳᵈ: My husband went back to work this day so we kept it simple and wrapped up a new board game and called it "Board Game Night". But it's also the Most Holy Name of Jesus, so it would be nice to incorporate that somehow.

Jan. 4ᵗʰ: Another birthday here. It's also St. Elizabeth Ann Seton's feast day. I had wrapped up the apple cider spices and a couple of books we haven't read in a while that the kids enjoy. We did "Apple Cider" night and made some popcorn & apple cider. We turned on the fireplace and read a couple of new stories.

Jan. 5ᵗʰ: Our gift exchange day. We give each of the kids a few dollars and each picks a sibling or parent's name out of a hat. We then go in and go shopping; we split the kids between us in such a way so they don't see their own gifts they are going to receive. I find that when they are allowed to buy each other gifts they get MORE joy out of giving than receiving. I think it's important for the kids to learn this at a young age, and to think about what their sibling wants, not what they want. The younger ones need help from me in this department. ☺ We did the shopping ahead of time but I think it would be neat to make today's box a hat with names in it. Then we shop, come home and wrap, and then that evening we open up all the gifts. It wasn't practical for us at the time; so we shop ahead and then put all the gifts in one big box for the day's opening.

Jan. 6ᵗʰ: Epiphany! Today I wrapped up some Christmas Carols I printed out. We sang Christmas Carols to Jesus and moved the Three Kings so they finally found Baby Jesus. This year we also want to actually PICK UP the blessed chalk from Mass and do the house blessing with it as well!

Every year is going to be different, but the idea behind it is to spend time as a family, teach the kids virtues, and really just focus on celebrating Christmas together with fun activities with more of a focus on Christ and the traditions of the Church. As the years go by I plan on trying to incorporate each feast day with our activity of the day, but that will come with time. Some other ideas I had that I didn't use yet but may this year: White Elephant Day (wrap something totally silly, could be combined with St. Stephen's Day); go to a park, sledding or ice skating depending on weather; Card game night; Make a blanket fort and read a story day; scavenger hunt day; game day with musical chairs and like games.

Christ is Born!

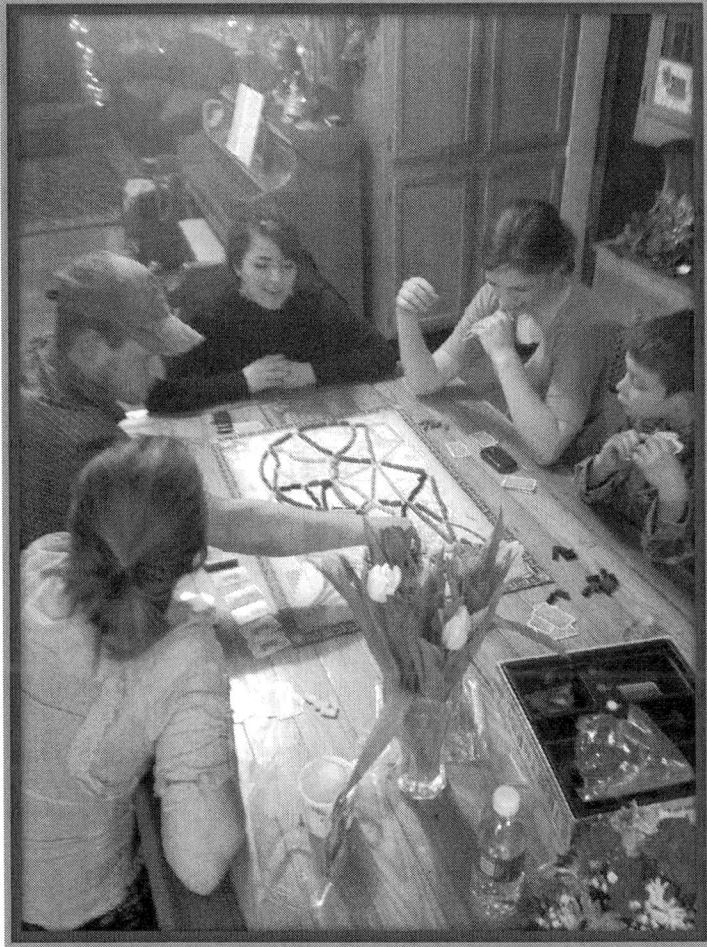

20. GEMS ON LOVING OUR GENTS

by Anne Joachim

The wonderful priest who gave us our pre-marriage instruction told us it would be the little things that make or break our marriage.

Remember….**Your hubby is number one** (After your faith, of course). **Your relationship takes work and sacrifice**. You can only change *yourself.*

Below are some final thoughts to leave you with this wonderful Christmas Season.

Do unto others….

We hear it a lot but it is profound. "Do unto others as you would have them do unto you." This goes especially for your spouse…..always **choose love,** *above all things.*

Don't sweat the small stuff.

Small irritations are not that important. We need to let them go. If we don't, they build up until they become a mountain that is hard to climb over. He doesn't take out the garbage? He is always late for dinner? He is always leaving things around? He goes hunting when you would rather he stayed home? Truly, these things are not important. Overlook them and get on to looking at his better side and being thankful! The rewards of a grateful heart are many!

The big stuff may take a little sweat.

There are sometimes big things that DO count. Don't push those ones down. Try to work these ones out. This can be difficult but it is worth it. The big things need to be dealt with or walls will begin to build between you both. Walls are not good and get thicker as the years go by. If talking to him about these things is not working, pray for a different solution. Our Lord will answer a sincere heart. Often the answers may be different than what we expect…so be open.

Greet him when he comes home with a loving smile.

A smile speaks volumes. Let your husband know you are happy to see him by smiling at him. Even when you are tired or have had a bad day. You want your husband to love coming home to you, don't you? Put your troubles aside just for a moment to make his day a wonderful one with a warm, loving smile. He probably didn't get a lot of smiles out there in the world, so let yours be one of the few and the very best that he can look forward to each day!

You need to make it a priority to pray for your hubby!

Every day you need to lift your husband up in prayer. Ask St. Joseph to help him to be a good husband and father. He needs you, who are his closest companion, to lift him up each day to our Heavenly Father. Ask Our Lord to protect him and to protect your marriage. What a wonderful gift a praying wife is!

Remember he's not your girlfriend.

This is important to remember. He doesn't always relate to the needs of a woman, so don't be unreasonable in your expectations. He won't always understand what you are feeling or what you are going through. He is different, he is a man. His heart and his mind work differently than ours. Don't demand that he be something he can never be.

Make him your best friend.

Friendship needs to be invested in. It needs to be worked on and nurtured. Do that for your most important relationship, your marriage. Find things you both enjoy and do those things. Talk, laugh, work and play together. Open up to him about your dreams….and make sure you ask about his own dreams.

Accept him….don't change him.

Remember why you married him. He has many good points and he is a good man just as he is. Yes, he has faults. Don't you? Leave the changing up to God. His work is way more efficacious than yours ever could be. Just. Love. Him.

Work on becoming a wiser woman each day.

Your husband relies on your wisdom. He would like to count on you for advice and insight. There are ways to give this advice…..learn how to do it so as never to offend. Wait to be asked.

Overlook his mistakes.

Of course your hubby will mess up sometimes. Is his communication lousy? Does he forget things that mean a lot to you? Does he not follow through? This all can be frustrating but we need to give him room to make mistakes, forgive him and love him anyway. Don't hold it against him. After all, he is human, like we are. ☺

Look for little ways to delight him.

Keep your eyes open for the little things that he appreciates. Does he like his clothes folded a certain way? Does he like it when you come to greet him when he gets home? Does he like his coffee cup warmed up before pouring? These may seem like small things but they say to him, "I care." Find ways to delight him…and Christmas is a great time to do those "little things"….but keep it up all year round!

❤ ❤ ❤ ❤ ❤ ❤ ❤ ❤ ❤ ❤ ❤ ❤ ❤

THE Time-Warp Wife

Marriage is a treasure. Guard it like one

21. SMORGASBORD 'N' SMIDGENS

A lovely stroll on a lovely day!

Theresa with her 2 little ones, Brendan and Sienna.

Virginia is our oldest and she is here with her husband, Vincent.

Here is the clan..... a new one, Nathaniel, has been added since then!

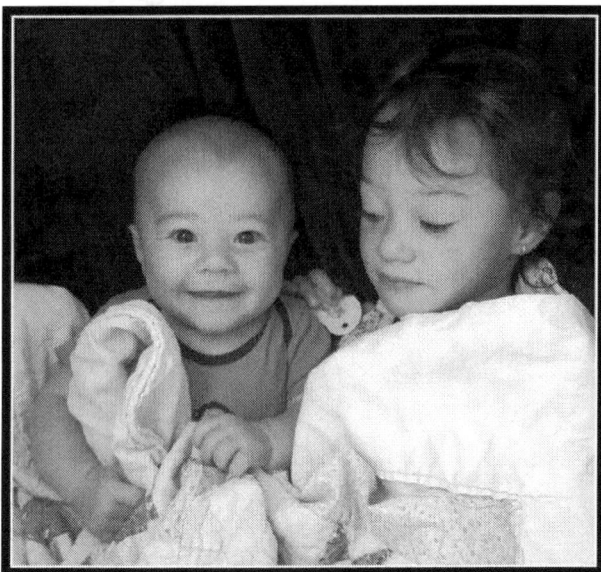

Nathaniel, the new addition to Vin & Gin' family. Cute, eh?

Our niece, Felicity, suffered through 2 weeks with us this September. She survived. :) She's pictured here with Hannah.

My oldest brother Mike and his lovely wife, Nellie. They visited this fall and were able to have some good times with Mom and Dad and all of us!

Nellie built some strong bonds while she was here.. They live in Kitimat, B.C., Canada. If you look on the map you will see that it is a long way from Kansas!

93

Praying the rosary on the street corner... the anniversary of the Miracle of the Sun in Fatima, Oct. 13th. Vinnie, our son-in-law, is leading the 15 decades.

May I ask WHY you are taking a picture of me???

Sometimes I wonder if it's his first love! ☺

Wonderful, (cheesy), grandchildren! These are all Virginia and
Vinnie's...Antonio, Benjamin, Johnathan and Emma.

L to R: Emma (Virginia's only girl...she has 5 boys) and Theresa's Sienna.

Lots of love to go around....that IS love, isn't it?!

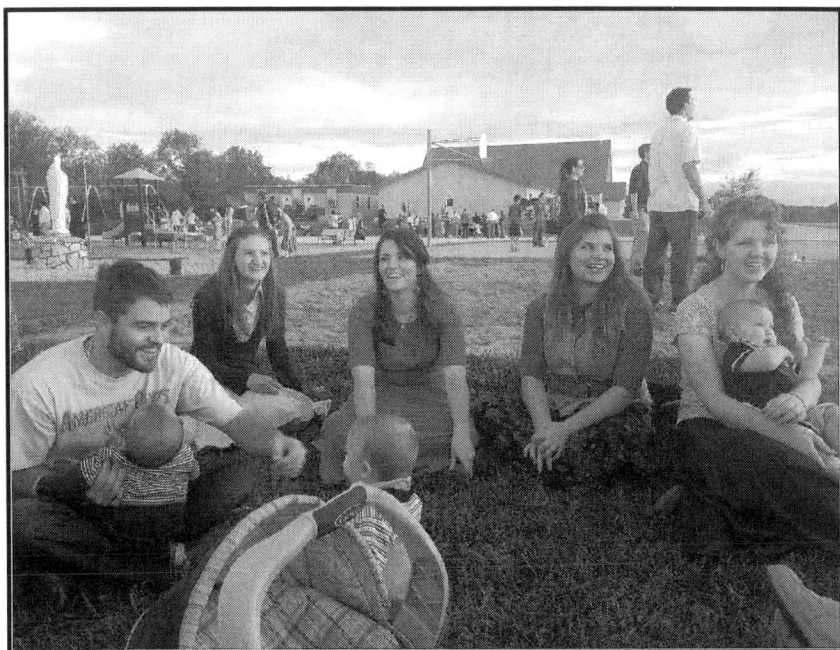

Good times at the September Annual Parish Picnic.

The hay ride is always a fun part of the Shibler picnic! It was pouring so we thought it would be canceled. The rain stopped and it proved to be perfect weather!

Margy, our 14 yr. old. She is running the house and making meals since Rosie has been sick.

Little grandsons pitching in!

Pumpkin time!

Getting ready for deer hunting season!

Rosie and Margy

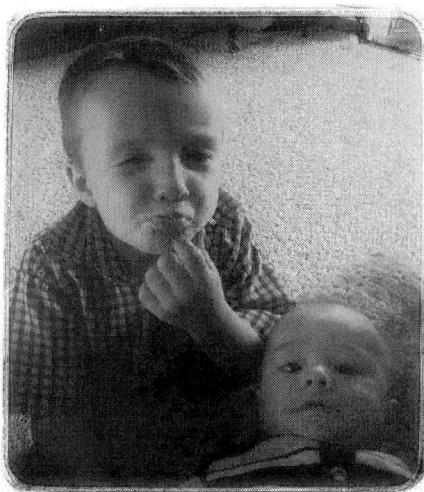

The thinker in Virginia's family....

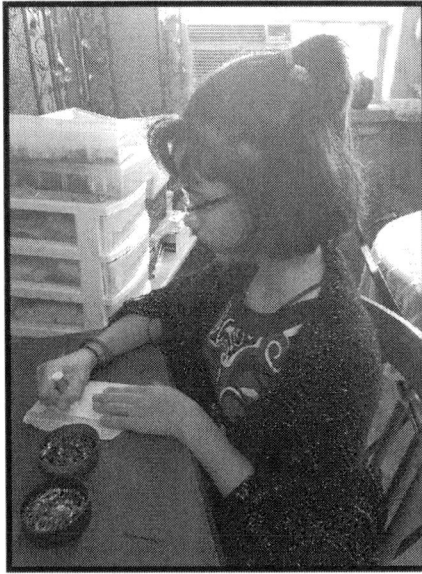

The intellectual in our family.

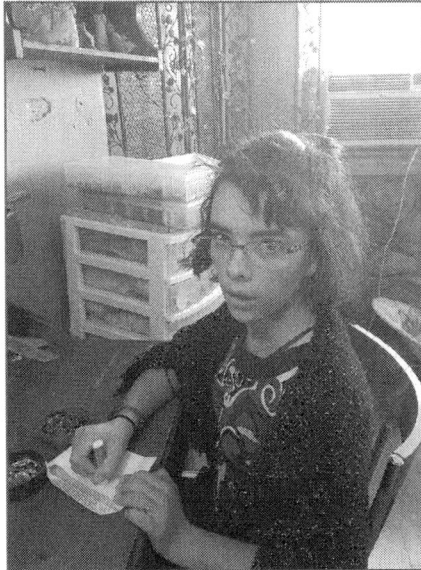

Okay, maybe not. Truth be known, Hannah's our creative one.

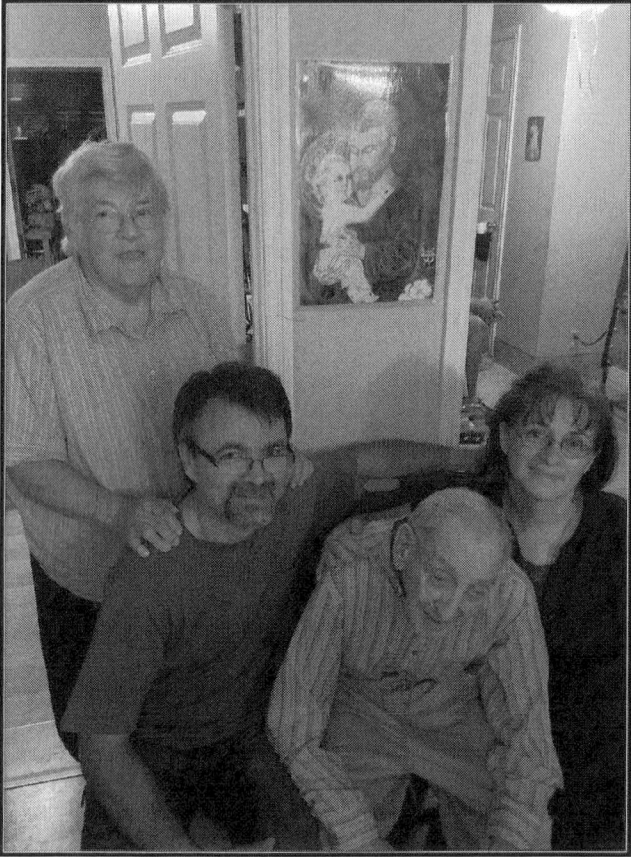

My mom, my dad, my big brother, Mike, and myself.

Colin (our second oldest son), Elizabeth, Jacob and Grace. They have a new addition since then...Isaac!

Rosie making cinnamon rolls.

Our good friend, Scott, moved here from up north. Here's his car. Have you ever seen anything like it? So many people were stopping and taking pictures that he put this sign on the back of it. It says, "Have you prayed lately?" ☺

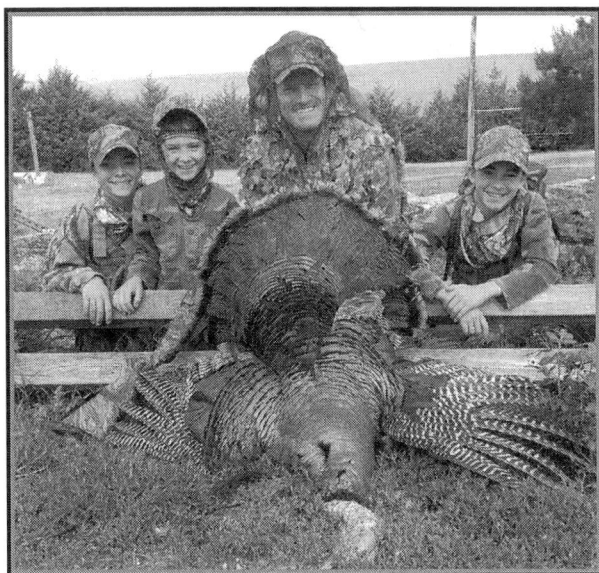

Here's Scott doing what he loves to do! The kids had a good time with him out in the woods at 3 am, rain coming down, shivering in their boots. Now THAT'S building memories!

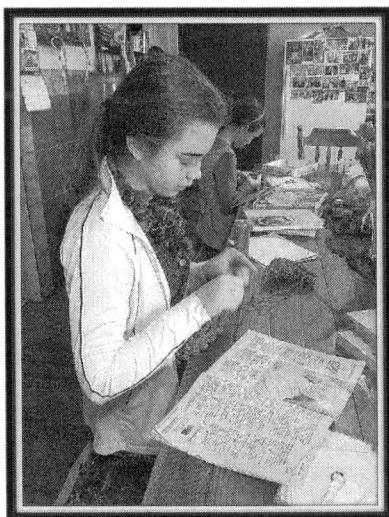

Margy, working on Christmas gifts.

Vincent's brother, Fran and his lovely wife, Lori with their family. These cousins are great buddies with our own kids!

Christmas fun with wonderful young people! These kids love their faith and are a joyful witness to it!

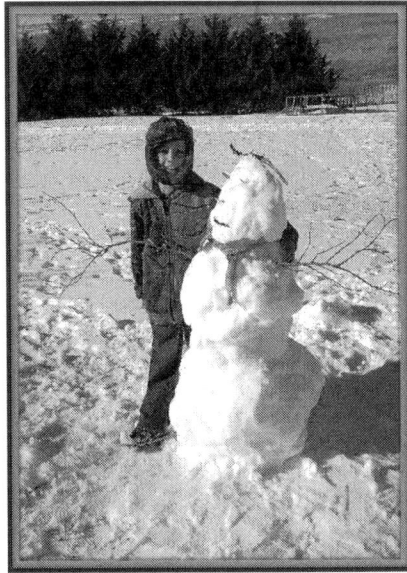

Snow doesn't last too long in Kansas, so you need to "make hay while the sun shines" or in this case, "make snowman *before* the sun shines!"

"The Rosary Maker's children have no rosaries"....when they make their own they do!

Merry Christmas from Hillarie George and Regina VanderPutten!

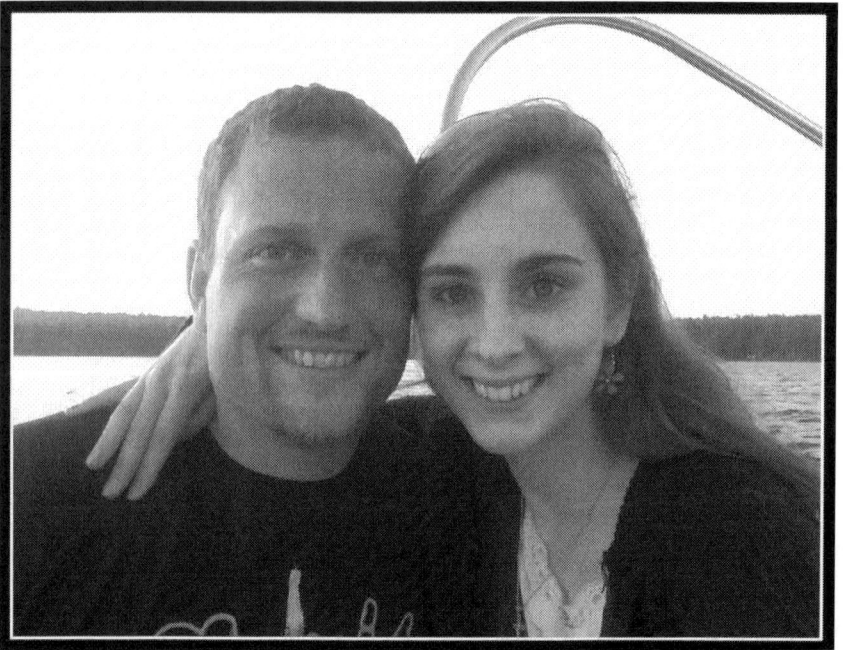

Merry Christmas from Mike and Jeanette Gallant!

And Merry Christmas from all of us!

MAY YOUR DAYS BE MERRY AND BRIGHT,

MAY YOUR FAITH BE A BEACON OF LIGHT!

To keep posted on upcoming issues of Finer Femininity Publications
subscribe to the email notifications at Finer Femininity Website:
www.finerfem.wordpress.com

To order more copies of this publication go to www.amazon.com

Or to www.meadowsofgrace.com

ABOUT THE AUTHOR

Hello! My name is Leane VanderPutten.

My family and I live in rural Kansas. Married 29 years, my husband, Vincent, and I have 11 children and 16 grandchildren. Our family strives to be faithful to Our Lord and His Church. We are devoted Catholics, homeschoolers, with 6 children still at home.

Our married children live nearby and we see our grandchildren often. Our family life is lively, full of faith and joy, with the occasional hardship sprinkled in.

My focus here, at **Finer Femininity,** is on the family — becoming the best possible wives and mothers. There is much in the church and in the world today to cause confusion and anxiety. We must bring up our children to thrive in a world full of this discord, with that inner peace only He can bring. This serenity is a fundamental part of the solution to all our troubles.

Here we learn ways to enhance our relationships. We learn about tweaking our attitudes. Often we need a paradigm shift in the way we look at circumstances to manage them in a manner more pleasing to God. The journey is uphill, sometimes rocky, often steep, but always edifying.

It is an inspiring work for me to share this information with all of you, and to reach more deeply into my own heart so I may change in order to become a better wife and mother, and especially, daughter of Him who sustains me every day on my journey.

May God bless us and Our Lady guide us as we endeavor to make this world a better place for our children and for our society, one day at a time.

Made in the USA
Charleston, SC
12 November 2014